blue
rider
press

THE MURDER OF SONNY LISTON

ALSO BY SHAUN ASSAEL

Wide Open: Days and Nights on the NASCAR Tour

*Sex, Lies, and Headlocks: The Real Story of Vince McMahon
and World Wrestling Entertainment*
(with Mike Mooneyham)

Steroid Nation: The Secret History of America's True Drug Addiction

THE MURDER OF SONNY LISTON

Las Vegas, Heroin,
and Heavyweights

SHAUN ASSAEL

BLUE RIDER PRESS

New York

blue
rider
press

An imprint of Penguin Random House LLC
375 Hudson Street
New York, New York 10014

Library of Congress Cataloging-in-Publication Data
Names: Assael, Shaun, author.
Title: The murder of Sonny Liston : Las Vegas, heroin, and heavyweights / Shaun Assael.
Description: New York, New York : Blue Rider Press, 2016. |
Includes index.
Identifiers: LCCN 2016016232 (print) | LCCN 2016028595 (ebook) |
ISBN 9780399169755 (hardback) | ISBN 9780698156661 (ePub)
Subjects: LCSH: Liston, Sonny, 1932–1970. | Las Vegas (Nev.)—History—
20th century. | Heroin—Nevada—Las Vegas—History—20th century. | African
American boxers—Biography. | Boxers (Sports)—United States—Biography. |
BISAC: SPORTS & RECREATION / Boxing. | BIOGRAPHY & AUTOBIOGRAPHY /
Sports. | TRUE CRIME / General.
Classification: LCC GV1132.L53 A88 2016 (print) | LCC GV1132.L53 (ebook) |
DDC 796.83092 [B] dc23
LC record available at https://lccn.loc.gov/2016016232
p.   cm.

Blue Rider Press is a registered trademark and its colophon
is a trademark of Penguin Random House LLC

ISBN 9780399169755

Printed in the United States of America
1   3   5   7   9   10   8   6   4   2

Book design by Gretchen Achilles

To David Larabell,

for taking me forward, to 1970

Sonny's the type of person that needs understanding. . . . He needs someone to help him control his emotion. He must be kept busy until all that youth and strength leaves him, like it leaves all of us.

—MONROE HARRISON,
Sonny Liston's original manager, in 1961

CONTENTS

THE
MURDER
OF
SONNY
LISTON

INTRODUCTION

On January 9, 1971, Geraldine Liston watched an overflow crowd at the Palm Mortuary pass by her husband's steel casket. The crowd comprised the business end of Las Vegas: showgirls, card dealers, casino execs, mob associates. Geraldine, her brown eyes hooded but sharp, studied their faces.

Some were there for the show. Stan Armstrong, a documentary filmmaker, would later recall walking a mile from his house at the age of fourteen because he knew the funeral of Charles "Sonny" Liston would be a piece of history. Others were there simply to be seen. Ed Sullivan, Ella Fitzgerald, and Doris Day sat in the front row while the Ink Spots did a special rendition of the 1966 hit "Sunny."

The last time Geraldine saw her husband alive, she was rushing to the airport to take their adopted son, Daniel, on a family visit to St. Louis. Even closing on fifty, Sonny still looked like he was meant for only one thing. He was built like a mushroom cloud, with coal eyes that had dead reckoning in them and monstrous hands that punched with the force of a government crash test.

When she returned home from her trip, Geraldine expected to find her husband planning his next fight or maybe playing craps with his best friend, Joe Louis. Instead, she followed the smell of rotting flesh to her bedroom, where she found his corpse slumped backward over their bed. So much methane had escaped up his legs that his penis was fully engorged and his testicles were the size of pool balls.

There was an era when Sonny terrified God-fearing whites by carrying the mantle of the angriest black man in America. But that time was long gone. Since the Beatles had put him on the cover of *Sgt. Pepper* and the Monkees had put him in a movie, he'd receded into a kind of genteel notoriety. Around Vegas, the restaurants comped him, the hookers waved as he passed by, and cops offered him rides home when he was drunk. He returned the favor by handing out preprinted business cards with his signature to tourists.

During his time in the spotlight, Sonny made it perfectly clear that he was willing to cheat on Geraldine whenever he had the chance. When a waitress presented them with a child that Sonny had fathered a few years before, Geraldine adopted the boy as her own, hoping he might finally give her the family she had always wanted. Sonny never became an ideal father, but his fragile fidelity always did lead him back home to her. And for that Geraldine remained his biggest defender. "He acts like he loves me, whether he does or not," she said. "He takes care of his home and that's all you can ask of a man."

On the night she found him, Geraldine let the police who were called to investigate do their work without helping too much. They walked past the stuffed bear in the living room that had Sonny's title belt wrapped around it, and into the den, where he kept his prized photos: the framed portrait with his arm around Lyndon Johnson; the one of him laughing it up with Sammy Davis Jr.; the sepia-toned keepsake of him mugging with Joe Louis when he took the crown from Floyd Patterson in 1962. The police rubbernecked, taking photos of themselves in front of the photos.

For all of its sophistication, Las Vegas was an unforgiving place in the 1960s, and it took a mean and unapologetic police force to hold it together. At the Greyhound station, plainclothes officers kept their eyes on the two-bit con men who rode in from wherever their last bit of luck had run out. As one deputy would say, "We had a blue binder book that had pictures of all the known career criminals. The sheriff used to tell us, 'If you kick their ass enough or throw them in jail enough, they'll leave town.' So whenever we saw somebody in that book, we found a way to kick their ass."

The town was deeply segregated, too. "If you were black and walking down the Strip just looking at the buildings and taking pictures, the sheriff's department would take you to jail," recalls Wilbur Jackson, one of the first African-American cops in the city when he was hired in 1958. "On the booking sheet, they'd write NOS." It stood for *Nigger on the Strip*.

In response, the residents of the Westside built their own shadow Strip along Jackson Street and filled it with rollicking jazz and bebop joints. But by 1970, Jackson Street had become a tapped-out vein running through the redlined heart of a ghetto.

Riots and civic neglect transformed the area into a badland where few without business dared to go. Sonny, of course, feared no one, and consequently made the Westside's best-known lounge, the Town Tavern, his home away from home.

On Christmas Day 1970, Sonny walked into the tavern with a white showgirl on each arm and ran into Clyde "Rabbit" Watkins, a former pool hustler who worked as a bellman at Caesars Palace. Watkins had met Sonny when he moved to town in 1966 and quickly became part of his entourage, jumping into Sonny's pink Cadillac when he wanted company and keeping an eye out when strangers started to get on the big man's nerves.

Watkins tipped the brim of his hat and wished his friend a Merry Christmas.

"What you doing later?" he asked.

"Coming to your house to eat," Sonny answered, laying his huge hands on Watkins's back.

To Watkins and all who saw Sonny that day, the champ was still a force of nature. Eight Christmases before, he had posed for the cover of *Esquire* in a red Santa Claus cap, looking every bit like an overgrown prison elf ready to shiv a reindeer. And as far as Watkins was concerned, little had changed. Sonny remained a menacing slab of manhood. Immutable. Impervious. Impossible. As a writer for *Sports Illustrated* once observed, "If [a] ship were going down, I would look at Sonny Liston to tell me what to do." So Watkins was shocked when he was working the night shift at Caesars and heard that the police were reporting Sonny was dead. As Watkins would recall it, he grabbed Joe Louis and Sonny's former manager, Ash Resnick, both of whom were on the casino floor, and ran red lights until they reached 2058 Ottawa Drive.

Geraldine was not happy to see Watkins. She wasn't blind to what her husband did, but she was old-fashioned enough to think that whatever it was should stay on the other side of town. Nor would she have been thrilled to see Resnick. He'd guided Sonny through his first fight against Muhammad Ali and it turned out to be the costliest loss of his career. Resnick was a player, and as far as Geraldine was concerned, Resnick had played them out of their retirement.

But what could she say about Louis? Joe had always been generous to Sonny and was probably his best friend in Las Vegas. The problem was that he'd also just been treated in a psychiatric hospital for a heroin addiction that made him delusional. They were a triangle without a steady side.

According to Watkins, the trio entered just in time to watch two medical examiners struggling to load Sonny into a body bag. He was just six-foot-one but he was thick, and the rigor mortis made him hard to lift. The coroners got him as far as the stairs when one of them slipped and sent the corpse sliding. It landed on the living room floor with a thud.

The Three Amigos stood over the body, slightly stunned. And as the house filled with cops, the last thing they needed to do was answer questions, especially after a sheriff's sergeant found a balloon of heroin on the kitchen table, below a wall phone. So they left.

The discovery of heroin led to a flurry of queries for Geraldine. What did she know about the drugs? Why had she waited three hours after walking through the door to report his death? What exactly did she find when she first got home? Was there any evidence of a struggle?

She waved off the questions, making it clear that she had nothing more to add that night. "Due to Mrs. Liston's *apparent* shock over the death of her husband," one officer wrote, "[we] were unable to interview her for further information."

She would keep whatever suspicions she had to herself until her death.

As Sonny's funeral wore on, Geraldine was consumed not only by who showed up but by who didn't. Her husband kept a large swath of his life a secret, and the people he kept in the shadows weren't about to show their faces now.

That included a well-known trumpeter who ran a drug gang and had hired Sonny to do collections for him with a .38 strapped to his ankle. The bandleader had a long track record with the cops and knew that they liked him for some part of Sonny's death, even if they didn't know what part yet.

And there was the beautician who dealt drugs out of the hair salon he ran across the tracks. He and Sonny did business together before they had a falling-out. Word on the street was that the beautician was looking for a piece of Sonny's scalp.

Even stranger was a milky alliance between a hero cop and an alcoholic grifter who became enmeshed in the darkest secret of Sonny's career: the circumstances of his first-round surrender to Muhammad Ali in 1965.

The Nation of Islam, meanwhile, lurked in the shadows, as worrisome an influence as it had been during that fight when rumors surfaced that its founder threatened to assassinate Sonny if he didn't take a dive. Ali was preparing to fight Joe Frazier for the biggest paycheck in the history of the sport, and Sonny was making noises that Ali owed him a piece of that purse as payment for taking a dive in '65, although that seemed to be news to Ali. The Nation's leaders had as much reason as anyone to make sure Sonny kept his mouth shut.

These were powerful people with means and connections, and they had all worried that Sonny was spiraling out of control. In her own way, Geraldine pleaded with him to slow down, enjoy life, and focus on raising their adopted son, who was all of seven. But whether it was because he was facing a midlife crisis or he simply thought no one could hurt him, Sonny couldn't take his foot off the gas. He'd always had a girl or four on the side, but he was risking more than usual this time around. He'd fallen in love with a buxom cocktail waitress who'd turned him on to heroin.

In what might have been the biggest threat of all, the feds were beginning to look into the source of the drugs he was buying and selling. An undercover agent had already met with him about doing a drug deal and there was every indication that Sonny was going to fall for the trap. There was no telling what he would do if he had to start wearing a wire on his friends. But it was hard to imagine anyone in Las Vegas who had a larger or more varied group of people who already wished him ill.

That's why those close to Sonny were skeptical when the coroner of Clark County issued a report that attributed his death to natural causes—specifically fluid on the lungs. It wasn't an uncommon way for a man of roughly fifty to die, especially since the underlying cause was ruled to be a lack of blood flow to the heart, a common affliction for people with hardened arteries. But Sonny was no ordinary man. As recently as his last fight, in June of 1970, his body looked fifteen years younger than his face, still massive and muscular. Among the fights he had won, nine of fifty-four had ended in the first round with victories and twenty-five others failed to go halfway.

"I knew the mortician who took care of Sonny," Rabbit Watkins would say in his Las Vegas home, not far from the Town Tavern, when I tracked him down more than forty years later. "He told me, from what he seen, that wasn't no natural causes."

The death of Sonny Liston remains one of the most enduring mysteries in Las Vegas. There never was a homicide investigation because his death was never classified as a homicide. As a result, leads surfaced that haven't been followed, suspects died with their secrets, and stories haven't been told.

At the funeral, Geraldine flung herself at her husband's casket and yelled, "I can't even see his face. Oh Jesus." Then she rose and shouted a question that would hover over the case for the next five decades. "Can you tell me what happened to you, Sonny?"

Part I

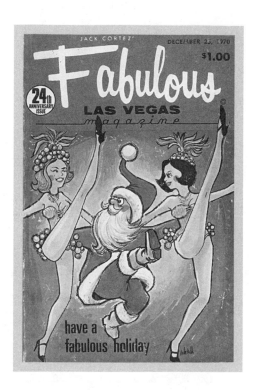

THE FRONT SEAT OF SONNY'S PINK CADILLAC

1.

HELLO, '70s

O n New Year's Eve of 1969, the casinos along the Strip pulled out all their stops to welcome in the new decade. For $19.70 per person, you could see Duke Ellington and his orchestra at Caesars for "the most fabulous new year's party in town." Not to be outdone, the Frontier featured Diana Ross in her farewell gig with the Supremes, and the Flamingo ran two all-nighters: Sonny & Cher performing twice in the main showroom—once at dinner and again at 2:15 a.m.—and a no-cover, dusk-to-dawn party downstairs in the Casino Theater with the Platters. Pearl Bailey was at the International, bringing her Broadway version of *Hello, Dolly!* to its main showroom, while Bobby Vinton and Don Rickles were at the Sahara and Shecky Greene was at the Riviera.

Las Vegas had never run so smoothly or so profitably. The *Sun* newspaper was so impressed with the way the casinos were vacuuming up tourist dollars, it boldly predicted that the cozy days of mob control were fading and a new era of corporate gaming was at hand. "Depending on who you talk to," the paper observed, "the corporations, with their businesslike efficiency, are either a black eye for the state or the salvation of Nevada gambling."

Frank Sinatra was the first one, really, to plant the idea of Vegas as a magnet for stardom. He reached the desert city in his prime, his golden voice a thing to worship up close. But the expectations of audiences were changing. In 1969, Elvis landed in a Convair jet to take care of business and proceeded to become the biggest nostalgia act along a Strip full of replicas. Now Las Vegas had become a place where you could earn top dollar on an edifice of familiarity. All you had to do was brush off the old act and play to people who didn't see you the first time around because they were busy raising the kids and putting food on the table.

One of the shrewdest judges of show business heat around, Merv Griffin, was bringing his CBS talk show to the Circus Maximus at Caesars and inviting the top names from each marquee as guests for a weeklong series he called "The Wonders of Vegas." Merv raved about the audiences and the resorts, but the twenty-eight-year-old pop star Paul Anka sounded an odd, discordant note. It had been a quarter century since Bugsy Siegel opened the Flamingo Hotel on Route 91 and changed the course of Vegas by ditching the old western pioneer motifs for glamour.

In the years since, the mob's money had built a luminous strip of playgrounds where the rich and infamous mingled, starting with the Thunderbird (1948), followed by the Desert Inn (1950), the Sands (1952), and the Riviera (1955).

Anka was just a kid when the last of them opened, but looking back, he'd write: "It was not uncommon to see Dean, Sinatra, and Sammy taking over from the dealers and handing out cards to the guests, visiting stars from L.A., high rollers, and so on. There weren't tourists in Vegas in those days the way there are today—it was an exclusive, elite group of people and the gaming areas were small."

By 1970 all that had started to change. Turning to Griffin's show audience, Anka said, "You know, Merv, it's not so glamorous anymore. It's getting very mechanical. As a matter in fact, all the excitement is disappearing."

Money, however, was gushing up from the desert. In January 1970, gaming revenues were up a robust 21 percent over the year before, to $44.9 million, and construction spending was rising fourfold. Much of that was due to the billionaire Kirk Kerkorian, who'd just opened the largest resort on the Strip—the 1,568-room high-rise International Hotel.

Everything about the thirty-four-floor mega-resort was gloriously overstated. On the top, Kerkorian created a glass-enclosed rooftop bar, the Crown Room, where "you couldn't be any higher." On the bottom he had a 350,000-gallon pool that was the largest in Nevada. A brochure for the hotel featured stylish couples living in the lap of this newly imagined luxury. "You never know whether you're going to sleep in Paris, or Rome, or

Hong Kong," it boasted, because each floor was done up in a different continental decor. Handling the luggage were valets dressed as French gendarmes.

Kerkorian spared no expense when it came to the entertainment, either. In the two-thousand-seat Showroom Internationale, a venue so majestic it took two kitchens to service, Elvis was playing twice a day, at six o'clock and midnight, and enjoying himself immensely. Still trim and square-jawed, his glint undimmed, he was on a pace to make $5 million for 1970, a staggering sum, and one he obliquely joked from the stage of the International was due to the Strip's new big-money bosses. Midway through his hourlong set, which included "Don't Cry Daddy," "Hound Dog," "Love Me Tender," "Kentucky Rain," "I Can't Stop Loving You," "In the Ghetto," and "Can't Help Falling in Love," he'd quip: "I'd like to get the guy who owns this hotel, that Kerkorian guy, in a craps game with Howard Hughes." Then he'd rip into a killer version of "Suspicious Minds."

Sonny Liston's name wasn't on any of the billboards outside the curved glass building. But he was part of the scenery just the same. In March 1966, Kerkorian gave the ex-champ a sweet deal on a nice little split-level with pool beside the Stardust Country Club, the same place where Debbie Reynolds once lived. Some said Sonny got a break on the $70,000 price tag as a payment for taking a dive in his second fight with Ali and making Kerkorian a lot of money. But hell, everyone had a theory about that fight. If it was fixed, it was the lousiest deal anyone had ever taken in boxing. A police report written long ago described a young Liston punching a man in the mouth and rifling through his pockets for six dollars. For all the distance he'd traveled, he was still fighting for chump change.

Still, Sonny loved Vegas, and the feeling was mutual. On April 5 of 1966, he drove his sleek new Cadillac convertible to the Clark County Sheriff's Office to announce that Las Vegas had a new resident. A clerk handed him something called a Convicted Persons Questionnaire, which every felon had to fill out, and he listed his height as six-foot-one, his weight as 220 pounds, and his occupation as a professional boxer. He also filled in the space that required him to note that he had been convicted of robbery in St. Louis sixteen years earlier and spent two and a half years in Missouri State Prison. And that was it, the end of the old Sonny and the beginning of the new one.

Every celebrity needs a hotel, and when Kerkorian's International opened in July of 1969, Sonny found a spot in the keno room and made it his base, showing up in shiny silver pants, polished black leather shoes, narrow sunglasses, and a black turtleneck that stretched against his massive chest. When fans came up to him while he was playing five-dollar blackjack and staring into his drink, he'd hand them cards with his name pre-signed on them so he wouldn't have to make eye contact.

But every so often a manager or a dealer would send someone over whom he would make eye contact with. At the bar, or in the bathroom, or in a leather chair in the lounge, the former heavyweight champion would unfurl his gigantic hand and inside would be cocaine.

Why was a world-renowned figure selling drugs? Everyone sold something in Vegas. But Sonny wouldn't even call what he was doing drug dealing. The real big mob guys came into town with hundreds of pounds of cocaine for the high rollers. Sonny was way, way downstream from that. His clientele was gym rats and hotel workers. Nonetheless, Sonny was involved deeply enough in the street scene to get caught up in a federal drug raid that nearly led to his being shot.

On February 19, 1969, Sonny's four title fights were well behind him and fans were paying to see a pale facsimile of the greatest jab in history. He hadn't been in the ring in four months—since he'd made a train wreck out of Amos "Big Train" Lincoln, a dubious heavyweight who was in a career free fall, at the Civic Center in Baltimore. And he wasn't due to fight again for another month, when he was scheduled to have a rematch against a soft-punching Cincinnatian named Billy Joiner. On that night, he told Geraldine that he was going out and he didn't know when he'd be back. He made his way in a pickup truck across the railroad tracks in Bonanza, to a place the cops pitilessly called Nigger Town.

His destination was a squat ranch home with a waist-high fence around it on the run-down corner of Duke Avenue and Castle Street that belonged to Earl Cage, a beautician who owned a salon, Earl's Beauty Cage. A roundish man with a pencil mustache and hair that was slicked back, Cage was no one's idea of a movie star, but he had a way with women—especially other men's wives. He'd massage hair relaxer onto their heads and while they were under his saucer-shaped dryers draw the blinds down over his door.

Besides selling hair straightening, Cage sold cocaine and heroin out of his back room. The samples he gave his clients were probably responsible for most of the sexual attention he received, but he also did a healthy business trafficking in felony weight, and that was what kept Sonny stocked in blow. On this night, a half-dozen people were inside the house when Sonny joined them and disappeared into a din of music. He missed the two cars filled with cops that pulled up to the corner.

Bill Alden, an agent for the Bureau of Narcotics and Dangerous Drugs, was behind the wheel of one of the cars. Alden had a photo of Cage and a layout of the home, and as he pulled to the curb he felt inside his vest for the arrest warrant that would let him break the door down. Once the two local cops who were trailing him parked their unmarked car and made their way to the back door, he made his way to the front. What happened next happened fast. He pounded on the door and yelled, "Police! You have ten seconds to open up." Having no faith that anyone would listen, he kicked the door off its hinges before he made it to five.

The interior had a small hallway that led to the living room on the left and two bedrooms on the right. Alden swept into one of the bedrooms, where he found Cage sitting on his bed, smoking dope with another man. The heroin dealer was surprised but apparently not too surprised, because he didn't resist. He stood calmly and allowed Alden to cuff him. This is going to be an easy night's work, the agent thought.

At that very moment, Alden heard a commotion in the next

room and the partner he'd brought along yell, *"Keep your hands up. Don't move. I told you to put your hands over your head!"*

Uh-oh. That was never good.

Making sure his prisoners were securely cuffed, Alden rushed into the next room to see Sonny advancing on his partner.

"I was a big boxing fan," Alden told me in his first-ever interview about the raid, whose details were conveniently left out of any police report and never made the newspapers. "I remember sitting in my car with my wife, who was my girlfriend at the time, and listening to the Liston–Patterson fight in 1962. I'd followed Sonny Liston through his whole career and there he was, standing right in front of me in a gray sweatshirt, giving me the same stare I'd seen so many times in photographs."

With Sonny refusing to back down, Alden had the sickening feeling that he might have to shoot the former heavyweight champion of the world. Just then, the two LVPD cops stormed through the back door and positioned themselves in front of Alden and his partner, blocking them from shooting as one approached Sonny and slowly said, "Okay . . . now . . . Sonny . . . Everybody's friends here. . . . Let's . . . just . . . cool . . . it."

"Friends here"? Alden thought. What the hell did that mean? "I don't know if he was under the influence, but he definitely didn't look like he wanted to be our friend," Alden told me. "If it went one step further, I would have shot him where he was standing."

Yet to his surprise, Sonny relented. He let the officer take him by the arm and guide him out the back door to his pickup truck, while Cage and everyone else in his house were cuffed. "We'll take care of him from here," the LVPD officer told Alden.

The reason Alden would remember the night in such detail was that it didn't end there. While Alden and his colleagues cuffed their suspects and brought them to federal courthouse to be arraigned, Sonny hurtled down Las Vegas Boulevard in his pickup, heading straight to a bar he knew on the north side.

A Las Vegas patrolman named Max Huggins happened by as Sonny parked in a no-parking zone and stumbled out. Huggins told me, "There was this kid from the PD, maybe five-foot-nine, not even 170 pounds. And he stopped Liston when he was drunk. He asked Sonny for his driver's license and Sonny took a swing at him and missed. The kid knocked him back, knocked him cold. A bunch of people rushed out of the bars when they heard the commotion. 'Hey, look, that's Sonny Liston.' That kind of thing. Sonny got arrested. But I'll tell you what, it went away fast." This is what was reported the next day:

SONNY LISTON POSTS BOND IN LAS VEGAS

Las Vegas, Nev. Feb. 20, 1969. [Reuters] Sonny Liston, former heavyweight boxing champion, today posted bond after being charged with driving under the influence of alcohol in northern Las Vegas last night. Liston, who was arrested while driving a pickup truck, will appear in court later this month.

Except that the case never went to court. In fact, the entire night seems to have been wiped clean. In later years, as Alden rose to one of the top jobs in the Drug Enforcement Administration, he'd remember thinking that Sonny must have had a guardian angel in the Las Vegas Police Department. "Why was he the only one let go?" Alden asked. "It didn't make any sense."

2.

PARADISE

The section of town that the Listons lived in, Paradise Palms, was the city's most exclusive enclave. Designed by a young architecture firm from Los Angeles, Palmer & Krisel, the Palms was envisioned as a place where the richest and most powerful people in Las Vegas could feel comfortable raising their families away from the chaos of the Strip.

Although Palmer & Krisel offered just a few basic models, they rotated the footprints of their lots so that adjacent homes stood at different angles. Three separate rooflines were offered as well: the futuristic butterfly design, with its two sides folded toward the sky like wings; the popular ranch; and the basic A-frame. Buyers could also customize their designs by picking different styles of decorative stonework, sanded stucco finishes, and carports instead of garages.

With lazy streets that ran in and around the Stardust Country Club, the Palms became a hit as soon as its first models were offered in 1963. Stanley Morgan of the Ink Spots had one of the A-frames down the street from Sonny at 1761 Ottawa, and a few houses in the other direction the legendary casino dealer Frank Masterana—a so-called mechanic because he was famous for helping the house cheat high rollers—had the butterfly roof. Donald Sutherland, coming off his huge success in *M*A*S*H*, lived in the L-shaped ranch on Pima Lane, while barely a mile away Howard Hughes's right-hand man, Robert Maheu, was raising his family in a split-level.

Sonny's model at 2058 Ottawa Drive was built on the sixteenth hole and was a mix of everything the development had to offer. Divided into two distinct halves, it had a spacious living area with a triple A-frame roofline connected by a narrow walkway to a modernist box with two bedrooms inside.

Even though Sonny wasn't much on golf, his neighbors got used to waving at him as he went on his morning runs. Geraldine became a familiar sight, too, gardening in the early morning or knitting by their pool. In time, she bought a swing set and other playground equipment so the kids in the neighborhood would feel comfortable coming over to spend time with Daniel.

The genius of Paradise Palms was that it offered the illusion of suburban living in a twenty-four-hour city where fathers got home at four or five in the morning with sex and booze on their breath. Kids still got put to bed after dinner and wives met to plan charity dinners. Everyone could at least pretend there were boundaries.

There was a great sense of the future in Paradise Palms but very little of the past. And that suited Sonny just fine. In the early 1960s the writer A. S. "Doc" Young took a tour of Sonny's birthplace in Forrest City, Arkansas, and described it as a place full of "wide, open spaces [where] there doesn't seem to be a whole lot stirring. . . . You notice these skimpy little houses . . . many with wrinkled, tin roofs; some set close to the highway, others dotting the vast acreage. The lawns are plain dirt and this is where little barefoot kids in their Lil' Abner clothing play."

Tobe Liston was a miserable miscreant of a man who rented the family's land from a sharecropper and gave away four-fifths of what he made farming cotton, corn, sorghum molasses, peanuts, and sweet potatoes. The only reason he even expended any sperm on Sonny, his twenty-fourth child in total and ninth by his second wife, Helen, was that he needed another hand to work his peanut and cotton fields. Because Forrest City did not require birth certificates, Sonny was born without even the most basic certification of his arrival, making the moment of his birth the first of many uncertainties that would shadow him through his life. A hard winter in 1942 left the Listons struggling to make ends meet and caused a fateful turn in their fortunes. "I could hear the news on the radio that help was needed in St. Louis and they'd pay you while you learned," Helen Liston told Young for his biography, *Sonny Liston: The Champ Nobody Wanted*. "So I went on up there and got me a job in a shoe factory."

Sonny had the biggest hands anyone in Forrest City had ever

seen. Had he stayed, he probably would have used them to kill his old man. Instead, he stole a few sacks of peanuts so he could buy a bus ticket to St. Louis to join his mother. "I figured it would be like the country," he'd say, "and all I had to do was ask somebody where my mother lived and they'd tell me she lived down the road a piece."

There was nothing criminally preordained about Sonny's arrival in St. Louis. The cops who found him sleeping in an alley fed him bologna and crackers and looked out for him the way cops used to do. As a family friend told Young, "They kept him with them for three days. They liked him—he did little chores around the station—and he liked them. He didn't want to leave." When the cops found Helen Liston living in the top two rooms of a house on O'Fallon Street, they reunited her with her son. Helen enrolled him in night school (not, as some cartoonishly suggested, an actual first-grade class) in the hopes that he could catch up on his education. But, as she conceded, "Charles didn't go like he should."

Instead, he gravitated to the street. "Someone would say, 'Let's stick up the restaurant,' and we did," Sonny would recall. "We just did the job like the stupid, crazy, bad kids we were." After a gas station heist in which two bystanders were mercilessly beaten, the St. Louis cops sent Sonny to the state penitentiary in Jefferson City.

Most people lose their livelihood when they go to prison, but Sonny found his. A prison chaplain who enrolled him in its boxing program was so impressed by his fearsome jab that he invited some local promoters to watch, and they in turn asked a local fighter to test the kid out. Before long, Sonny had been paroled into their custody and a new life.

"The boy still is crude; he's no Joe Louis yet," the head of the St. Louis Golden Gloves team observed. "But he's much faster on his feet and has more speed than Louis had at his age." After he captured the national Golden Gloves title in 1952, the *St. Louis Globe-Democrat* raved, "Charles (Sonny) Liston, besides being the most powerful man ever to come out of the Golden Gloves here, has the unique ability to be able to stand up under a punch that would ordinarily stagger a water buffalo."

Back then, while he was still making $35 a week, Sonny couldn't have conceived that his ability would take him to a place like Paradise Palms.

"Nobody don't want a bum," he once said, remembering his time on the streets. "Down there is a lonely place. There ain't nobody going to leap down and say, 'Hey, fellow, want a hand?' Not for me there wasn't, anyways."

Of the many crossroads in his life, the one that may have meant the most came in 1956, while he was climbing the heavyweight rankings. Sonny was at a party with Geraldine and called a taxi to take them home. When he walked out and saw a St. Louis cop ticketing the taxi, he shouted, "Hey, why don't you lay off."

"How about you mind your business or I lock you up," the cop fired back. Or at least that was what Sonny said when he explained why he'd lifted the officer to shake loose his gun and, in the process, set him down awkwardly and broken his leg. The officer's version was more sinister. He accused Sonny and an accomplice of dragging him into an alley and stealing his weapon. As the officer wrote in his report, "I hollered, 'Don't shoot me.' Liston let up and then hit me over the eye with either his fist or the gun. Then they ran up the alley."

Blacks from the bleak coal-soaked slums rallied around Sonny. And they weren't alone. Even the staid *Saturday Evening Post* questioned the officer's story, wondering why he didn't just write the ticket and walk away. Not that the cops in St. Louis cared. They made Sonny's life hell, stopping him by his own estimation "fifty or a hundred times" and padding his rap sheet with busts. The punitive overcharging became self-fulfilling when he was sentenced to nine more months behind bars.

It's hard to overstate the crossroads that lay before him when Sonny was released. The Montgomery Improvement Association had recently named a twenty-seven-year-old doctoral student in theology, Martin Luther King Jr., as its minister. There was room for all sorts of new leaders. But in 1957, Sonny's mob handlers in St. Louis decided to sell his contract to a pair of tough-talking crime bosses in Philadelphia, and there was no turning back.

His life since then had been one investigation after another and a constant drumbeat of criticism that he was a linchpin between boxing and the mob. But to look at Sonny in Paradise Palms was to see the payoff from that lifetime of beatings.

He owned a thin metal card that got him into a golf course clubhouse where gin and tonics flowed freely in the early afternoon, helping the normal boundaries of celebrity fade into a well-heeled kind of bonhomie. After playing eighteen holes of golf, the members of the Rat Pack might have a drink or two and chat with their less famous neighbors, generally casino executives or mobsters whose kids played on the streets and lawns, blithely unaware that everyone didn't live with Frank Sinatra winking at them from the fourth fairway.

In a town of two and three shows a night, everyone was on their second or third acts. There were no judgments, or at least none that really mattered. The Las Vegas patrolman Max Huggins would remember making his rounds through Paradise Palms when a woman who lived on Ottawa Drive pigeonholed him to complain about the loud parties that Sonny threw when Geraldine was away. They were raucous affairs in which friends from the Westside and boxing associates mixed with showgirls and comics like Redd Foxx, Slappy White, and Nipsey Russell.

"He's a goddamn drunk," she complained. "He's going to die in the gutter."

Huggins thanked her for her concern and walked off. Everybody had the same thing said about them at one time or another in Paradise Palms.

On February 21, 1969, the *Sun* reported the arrest of Earl Cage on the front page without any mention of Sonny at all.

Instead, the story focused on an eighteen-year veteran of the Las Vegas PD, John Sleeper, who green-lighted the raid. A large man with slits for eyes and wishbone eyebrows that crept up when something struck him as suspicious, Sleeper was perfectly suited to the task of running the vice unit for a force of five hundred men that covered the fifty-three-square-mile city. He had thin, pursed lips, a strong sense of Mormon rectitude, and the ability to inspire fierce loyalty among the agents he handpicked.

Even though he wore a flattop and rarely allowed himself to be seen out of uniform, Sleeper encouraged his men to grow their hair and pose as hippies or bikers so they could blend into the most dangerous parts of the city. Then he'd throw parties after busts at his house, where he handed out long-neck beers and turned Hank Williams way up loud. His sense of bravado was such that when a recalcitrant drug dealer refused to move from his corner, he asked, "Don't you know who I am?" and opened his leather jacket to reveal a T-shirt emblazoned with a Superman logo. "I'm Super Narc!"

Sleeper claimed to loathe politics but he was a cagey tactician who was determined to close what he perceived as a prestige gap with the Clark County Sheriff's Department, which had responsibility for all of Clark County's unincorporated areas, including the hotels and casinos on the Strip. He also couldn't wait to take credit for Earl Cage's arrest, which might not have been the smartest thing to do.

Cage had been arrested on a federal warrant and arraigned in federal court, which left him thinking that the feds had set him up. But there was Sleeper, bragging that he was actually the brains behind it all. For Cage, a man with an unforgiving and violent reputation, it wouldn't have taken a lot to conclude the same thing that Bill Alden, the federal agent who'd nearly shot Sonny, had concluded: that the champ had had something to do with setting it all up.

In the fall of 1969, Richard Nixon was under siege for his role in expanding the war in Vietnam. *The New York Times* had exposed the secret bombing of Cambodia, and antiwar protests were breaking out all over the country. On June 27, in what became a signature turning point for public opinion, *Life* magazine had published the faces of 242 servicemen who had been killed the prior week, causing shocked Americans to confront the once smiling faces of the dead. With a siege mentality already settling in, Nixon convened a crisis group headed by his attorney general, John Mitchell. Reminding the room that Nixon had run on a law-and-order platform, Mitchell asked his aides how they could deliver on that promise and at the same time distract America from the war in Vietnam. When someone suggested the drug issue, the attorney general took his pipe out of his mouth and said, "I like it."

In the first battle of that war, Nixon targeted the drugs that were coming over the Mexican border. Mexico's government was reluctant to crack down on peasant farmers who grew marijuana for the cartels, and in what became known as Operation Intercept, two thousand agents were dispatched to the border to stop every car trying to get into the United States. In foreign policy terms, it was a debacle. While Mexican citizens sweltered in their cars in hundred-degree heat, Mexico's president accused Nixon of creating a "wall of suspicion" and warned of reprisals.

This new drug war was the best thing that could have happened to John Sleeper. Drug prices started skyrocketing in what the *Sun* called "the current state of bedlam brought about by the federal Government's Operation Intercept." When the Nixon administration began sending grants to police departments, Sleeper suddenly found himself with a windfall to expand his small vice unit. He doled out money to informants up and down the city to create a spy network and pressed his friends in the casino world to let him know when big-time traffickers were staying in their high-roller suites.

Aided by the federal Bureau of Narcotics and Dangerous Drugs, which helped him with cash to finance his drug buys, Sleeper began expanding his undercover operations. He even took a page from the hit show *The Mod Squad* by posing his young detectives as hippies or high school seniors so they could spy on protest organizers in the schools. If that put him on a collision course with the county's powerful sheriff, Ralph Lamb, well, Sleeper didn't care. In fact, he couldn't wait for a showdown.

3.

LOST VEGAS

S onny's head kept telling him that he should stay in Paradise Palms and keep Geraldine happy. But his heart kept leading him to the boozy, shiftless soul of the Las Vegas ghetto.

Most of the African-Americans who lived in the Westside had relatives who arrived in the teeth of the Great Depression. They gave up making $2.50 a day farming in Louisiana, Arkansas, or Texas so they could start new lives by laying the brick and mortar that built the casinos. By the early fifties, a second wave followed to fill the jobs that the new casinos had available for kitchen help, shoe shiners, janitors, and, of course, showgirls and musicians.

They settled in shacks and, if they were lucky, worked for employers who ran shuttles to the casinos, because it was a dangerous trip to make on foot. Gauntlets of white toughs often waited on the other side of the tracks to cause trouble. Sunday was the only day when a family dressed for church could feel halfway comfortable venturing into the white side of town and walking past the shops and casinos that they were barred by law from entering.

Walled off and hemmed in, the residents of the Westside built a city within their city and filled it with family-owned businesses: Johnson's Malt Shop, the Dixie Meat Market, Crockett's barbershop, and of course Gilbert's Liquor Store, where old man Gilbert was willing to sell whiskey on credit.

In the middle of it all was the beating heart of their neighborhood: The shadow strip that ran along Jackson Street was luminously filled with nightclubs that jumped all through the night: the Cotton Club. The Ebony Club. El Morocco. The Louisiana Club. Town Tavern. After the casinos on the white side of town closed, their headliners would come to Jackson Street to unwind. Kids who couldn't go inside hung out on the street, hoping to catch a glimpse of the stars.

The pivotal moment for the Westside came in 1955, while Sonny was still slugging his way through St. Louis. A group of white investors from Los Angeles sensed the time was ripe for something grand and opened an integrated hotel and casino, the Moulin Rouge, that rose fifteen stories over Bonanza. Its location, a stone's throw from the railroad tracks, lured adventurous whites to gamble in its casino, chase colored showgirls, and rub shoulders with black entertainers, who loved playing the place, since it afforded them accommodations they couldn't get anywhere else. (In one famous story, Nat King Cole was allegedly barred from entering the Tropicana by a doorman who told Cole's white companion, the publicity manager of the Sands, "I don't care if he's Jesus Christ, he's a nigger and stays out.")

In just a few short weeks, the hotel became more successful than its investors ever envisioned. In fact, it became *too* successful. The *Sun* wrote about the "factions in town that will not stop to wreck the experiment of the Moulin Rouge," which was diverting business from Strip stalwarts, like the Sands and the Sahara. Six months after it opened, it was padlocked in a cloud of confusion.

There was talk that the big hotels pressured the banks to call in its loans, that the original investors were stretched thin, that the mob was skimming its profits. As dancer Norma Tolbert later recalled, "We thought it would last forever, [but] we showed up for work one day and it was closed."

With an unlit sign casting shadows on an empty parking lot, the Moulin Rouge became an ugly symbol of crushed aspirations. By the time Sonny arrived a decade later, the Westside was a ghost of its former self. Still, it offered him its own kind of sanctuary. On the white side of town, he always found himself on guard, either from the curiosity seekers who wanted to poke him like some goddamn zoo animal or from the good-natured liberals who wanted to tell him they understood his pain. (He couldn't tell who was more irritating.) On the Westside he didn't have to put up with any of that.

One of Sonny's favorite places was Loves Cocktail Lounge, a cozy spot on Jackson Street with leopard-patterned couches up front, a long bar that seated fifty, and a poolroom in the back decorated with photos of all the celebrities who stopped in. The list included B.B. King, Michael Jackson, Big Joe Turner, and Cassius Clay.

To hear the lounge's owner, Dorothy Love, "Once Sonny got drunk, there was no one nicer. He completely forgot who he was. He'd buy drinks for the room and all our regulars gathered around him. Someone would say, 'Tell us how you knocked out Floyd Patterson,' and he'd get up and, you know, box with them. He'd keep the whole room laughing. A lot of nights I brought him over to our house and cooked him neck bones and gravy. He was a member of our family."

It's a heartfelt story with a few unintended insights. The idea of sitting at home with Geraldine must have been so painful for Sonny that he needed to sit at a bar among strangers and tell the same stories over and over, even as his wife and adopted son sat at home watching *The Johnny Cash Show* or *Here's Lucy* on their new color television.

If he wasn't at Loves, he'd be at a dingy place down Jackson Street, Low Cost Card Games, playing a fast, betting version of rummy called Tonk. Or at Friendly Liquor, a packaged-goods store on the edge of the Golden West Shopping Center that had a bar with about ten stools where he could keep an eye on his pink Cadillac outside.

What bothered the churchgoing leaders of the Westside

about Sonny's outsize presence wasn't that he was drinking but that that was pretty much all he was doing. "I was very involved in the women's group of the United Methodist Church," Ruby Amie-Pilot, a prominent member of the NAACP, told me. "With all the problems going on, he could have made a choice to be involved. But I didn't know of his involvement in any of the groups I worked with." When asked if she ever met Liston personally, the longtime activist added, "No, I didn't want to cross him."

Wilbur Jackson had no such qualms. A lifelong resident of the Westside, the Las Vegas policeman understood as acutely as anyone how the racial lines cut. "If I was on the white side of the underpass at Main Street and Bonanza, I couldn't make an arrest," he told me. "I had to wait to go to the black side before I could enforce the law."

Jackson's visibility, and his full-throated support of the NAACP, made him a leading voice in the community. There weren't any streetlights in the area he patrolled, and the police department didn't have walkie-talkies or radios. So Jackson walked his beat alone, measuring out a circular section from Gilbert's Liquor Store at Bonanza and D, up to H Street and the El Rio Club, over to Lake Meade Boulevard and then back to Jackson Street. If he got in trouble, the only way he could call for help was on the pay phone at the Rancho Market.

That prominence led to a call one day from a young Clay, who wanted to know if he could walk the beat with Jackson. The two men spent the night talking about Clay's emerging conviction that America's blacks needed to take their affairs into their own hands.

One of the places where Jackson liked to stop after his late-night shifts was the Cove Hotel on Jackson Street. The Cove was an example of the racial schizophrenia in the city. Even though its clientele was all black, the Cove took out ads in the local papers featuring a white bodybuilder on a surfboard, in the hopes that banks that didn't normally lend money to African-American businesses would be tricked into thinking it catered to Caucasians. Its list of advertised amenities included "air conditioned rooms, heated pool and sunbathing, surf room, lounge and bar, dancing, entertainment, banquets, conventions."

Jackson enjoyed the girlie dance reviews and found himself one evening standing behind a table by the stage. He had no idea that Sonny was sitting in front of him until the crowd pressed toward the stage and he bumped into Sonny's elbow. With surprising speed, Sonny wheeled around and motioned as if he was about to grab Jackson and throw him across the room.

At six-foot-three, Jackson wasn't the kind to back down easily. He took out his Smith & Wesson and leveled it at Liston's head. Sonny, who kept a gun strapped to his ankle, glared at Jackson. But the showdown ended there. For whatever reason, Sonny chose not to be another headline on this night.

"He liked to push people around, but he wasn't the baddest man on the Westside," Jackson recalled. "He wasn't no Cassius Clay in our community. He knew who I was and knew he'd made a mistake. So he went back to his drink and I went back to the show."

The Golden West Shopping Center was another good intention gone wrong. The leaders of the Westside hoped that if they built it, investment would follow. But thanks to the dire shape of the neighborhood, that investment never came. Instead, zombie armies of junkies shuffled up and down its parking lot, providing an open market for drugs.

Friendly Liquor Store, which was across the street, got the spillover. "It was bad, real bad," recalls former Las Vegas PD narcotics officer Joe Crocetti. "People who'd kill you for a dime and slice you open hung out there. I remember we got a call about a fight, and six of us showed up in one car with shotguns. When I walked in, a guy was literally holding his intestines in his hands. Somebody had sliced him. You couldn't see stuff like that in the movies."

Sonny liked Friendly's because it gave him a chance to see and be seen. Anyone who wanted to buy drugs knew where to find him, and he knew where to find anyone who owed him for them. But in the fall of 1969 it also provided a perch to watch his playground burn.

The spark was a common traffic stop. A black police officer, Robert Arrington, was patrolling the area when he stopped a cabdriver, who was also black, for speeding. The commotion caused two brothers to come running run from their house, and when Arrington told them to go back inside, one returned with a shotgun. Arrington sprayed him with Mace and called for backup, but by the time the brothers were in cuffs, a crowd of 150 onlookers had gathered, some advancing on the officers and pelting them with rocks before they splintered into packs and began fanning into the night.

Small clusters of chaos turned into larger clusters as fires spread through street corners and tinderbox tenements. More than two hundred cops flooded the area before the chief of police decided that was making matters worse and pulled them shortly before midnight. By dawn, city officials were holding their breaths and calling the episode an isolated outbreak.

Later that afternoon, however, two white men picking up a friend at Golden West were set upon by a gang and beaten unconscious, sparking a second wave of violence that was twice as fierce. This time rioters swarmed the shopping center, looting Friendly's for liquor bottles so they could make Molotov cocktails. A sixty-four-year-old electrician was pulled from his vehicle and beaten while a woman was yanked out of hers and forced to strip. Several bystanders were wheeled into emergency rooms with their heads cracked open. Cars were set on fire and the windshields of passing police cruisers broken.

This time every cop in the city was pressed into action. Even plainclothes detectives who looked more like the rioters than cops were ordered to don their uniforms and report to a command station with their helmets on and nightsticks at the ready. The Golden West looked like the Alamo as sharpshooters were stationed on rooftops and police cruisers formed barricades. When a 7:00 p.m. curfew was imposed, commanders started shouting through bullhorns: "Those who don't want to get hurt should leave the area immediately." In a questionable decision, the fire chief, Jerry Miller, recalled all his trucks out of what he insisted was fear for the safety of his men. By nightfall the power company had even turned off electricity to the area.

"They wouldn't let nobody in and they wouldn't let nobody out," Wilbur Jackson recalls. "[People] couldn't go to work on their jobs, and say if somebody was on dialysis or a breathing machine or something, the power was cut off. I'd never heard of nothing like that in law enforcement. And the thing was, it was the kids who were rioting. The people in the community didn't have nothing to do with it. Folks like me wasn't running through Golden West Plaza setting fires and stuff."

When those fires were finally put out, the Westside was in ruins.

If the melee showed anything besides how easily poverty burns, it was that there was a militant army that wasn't going to be satisfied with the old-timers in the churches who were counseling patience. A mimeographed newsletter, *The Torch*, warned: "Don't be too damn surprised if we ignore your racist bureaucracy in the future. We are telling it like it is. Dig it. You will reap what you have sown. And, baby, it's liable to be one hell of a harvest."

Community leaders like Jackson and Ruby Amie-Pilot desperately tried to pick up the pieces. They held meetings with elected officials to open lines of dialogue. But both told me that every time they saw Sonny after that, they couldn't contain their contempt. It wasn't just that he seemed to disregard the decades of history that had been destroyed around him. Or that he drank to excess and pumped drugs into an already sick bloodstream. It was that he did all of it knowing he could return to his pretty little house in the suburbs anytime he wanted. "The rest of us, we stayed," Jackson said.

Of course, Sonny looked at it differently. He'd done plenty for the movement. In fact, he might say that he'd taken more punches than any of them.

Back in 1960, when he was the leading contender for Floyd Patterson's crown and found himself in the middle of a national debate about whether he was civilized enough to fight for the title, Sonny felt humiliatingly exposed. His arrest and jailing for breaking the cop's leg in 1956 cemented his reputation as a man at war with the world around him, while a December 1960 appearance before a U.S. Senate committee reinforced the perception of him as uneducable.* "How much education did you get?" the Democratic senator from Tennessee, Estes Kefauver, asked once Sonny was sworn in.

"I didn't get any," he replied

"You didn't go to school at all?"

"No, sir. Too many kids."

"How many kids were there?" the senator asked.

"Well, my father had twenty-five."

---

*In his book *The Phantom Punch*, Rob Sneddon noted that an investigator for the committee leaned over to Liston and said, "You see that briefcase over there? It's all Sonny Liston and it's all bad."

"Did you have to work to help support the other twenty-four children?"

"That's right," Sonny said.

"What did you do?"

"Pick cotton."

"Do you read at all?"

"No, sir," Liston replied, "I don't."

"Do you sign your name?"

"Yes, sir."

"Can you sign your address?"

"No, sir."

"Suppose your share of a fight purse was $25,000 and they handed you a check for it," Kefauver asked. "Could you tell whether they were giving you a check for $25,000?"

"Not exactly."

"You would have to depend on somebody else?"

"Yes, sir."

Not long after that, Kefauver got around to Sonny's mob promoter, Frank Carbo, whose links to the Lucchese crime family were infamous. "Do you think that people like [Carbo] ought to remain in the sport of boxing?" he asked.

"I wouldn't pass judgment on no one," Sonny replied in his best church manner. "I haven't been perfect myself."

There wasn't a soul in the press who didn't feel free to weigh in on his performance. In Pittsburgh, the *Courier* newspaper asked its readers, "Should Liston's police record keep him from boxing professionally?" and answered with a survey in which its black readers uniformly answered, "No."

Sonny tried to climb the ladder of the educated Negroes who seemed to hold him in contempt. Really he did. He worked with the *Chicago American* on a profile in which he tried to appeal to the black upper class. After admitting that he had hung out with "some pretty tough men" in his St. Louis days, he said: "I never knew there were any other kind of people. I'd heard of Negro doctors and lawyers, and outstanding businessmen, of course. But how was I going to get with them? They were educated, refined people. I wasn't educated and I knew I wasn't refined."

When Patterson finally agreed to a fight in 1962, it was as if he'd agreed to an act of supreme charity instead of acknowledging the very great challenge before him. Jackie Robinson said it was a shame that Liston's "record isn't better" but placed the pressure on Patterson, saying he had to fight Liston "to prove himself to the public." The activist Dick Gregory insisted that the problem wasn't that Liston's influencers were mob-connected; it was that they were white. John F. Kennedy urged Patterson to find someone with a better "character."

Liston's *character*, in other words, had become a national obsession, a laser light on the issue of whether the fight for civil rights needed to be waged with civil behavior. Dr. King was busy promoting the philosophy of nonviolence that he'd traveled to India to study in 1959, and the Freedom Riders were launching their first foray into the South. Yet here came the most violent man on the planet, demanding to take one of its most symbolic crowns.

When Sonny wrested the title away from Patterson at Comiskey Park in Chicago on September 25, 1962, he was surprised by the weight that settled on him. He had won it in two minutes and five seconds—the first time a heavyweight crown was decided in the first round—starting with a right uppercut, continuing with two left hooks, and finally, when Patterson used his left hand to rest on the ropes, a pile-driving left hook to the jaw. But the press acted like Sonny had robbed a bank. Even when Sonny suggested that a rematch should be held under the auspices of Big Brothers "to prove that I mean what I say about helping boys who need help," Larry Merchant of the *Philadelphia Daily News* suggested that he get a ticker-tape parade made out of arrest warrants.

On the way back to Philadelphia, Sonny began practicing a speech about how he, like Patterson, would reign as a gentleman champion. When he walked off the plane in Philly, only a ground crew was there to hear it.

Fuck it, he thought, turning his back on the city that turned its back on him. He packed up his things to drive cross-country with Geraldine, telling the press, "I'd rather be a lamppost in Denver than the mayor of Philadelphia." Unfortunately, the Philly cops gave their Denver brethren such an earful about him that he couldn't get any more peace when he arrived in Colorado. He was rousted, arrested, and generally made miserable. "Sonny got stopped every day for about twenty-five straight days," an old sparring partner, Ray Schoeninger, told *The Denver Post*. "We used to go do our road work at the City Park Golf

Course. Sonny used to drive this big, fancy Cadillac and the cops would just wait for him to get on the road. Then they'd pull him over, just to see his driver's license. Just to hassle him."

Fearing that time was running out to get him in shape for his rematch with Patterson, his mob handlers shuffled him off once more, this time to train in Las Vegas.

Vegas! Why hadn't he thought of it before? By day he opened up his workouts to high rollers. At night there was an institutional supply of showgirls. Sonny was in the best shape of his life when Patterson showed up to the rematch at the Las Vegas Convention Center on July 22, 1963, and this time was only able to hang in the ring for four more seconds than the first time. After the clouds of defeat cleared from his head, Patterson walked to his dressing room and told reporters that he was going to have to start all over again. What choice did he have?*

While Patterson was left to rebuild his career, Sonny became the subject of ever greater caricatures. Press conferences became exercises in trying to get the big oaf to blow his stack. Mark Kram of *Sports Illustrated* got under Sonny's skin by going to City Hall in Denver, looking for police records. "You been checkin' up on my record," Sonny exploded at him. "Do you believe in Jesus Christ? Ya ever hear people talk about him? If they gonna talk 'bout him, they gonna talk 'bout me. Why, poor

---

*Patterson won his next five fights, earning a title shot against Ali in 1965 that was overshadowed by a back injury that he'd suffered in training. He managed to eke out twelve rounds, but thanks to Ali's taunting and his own diminishing skills, he was never the same after he got knocked out. He fought sixteen more times in seven years, going 12–3–1 and ending his career in 1973 with a losing rematch against Ali at Madison Square Garden. In his later years, battling Alzheimer's, Patterson reflected on his fame by saying, "I wanted to be with people. To laugh and enjoy and talk with them. I didn't enjoy being special."

old Joe Louis, a wonderful guy like him, they even talked about him. You know they gonna talk about me. Oh, man. Someday I gonna write a book, and I gonna talk about some people."

Sitting down to write his piece, Kram quoted the entire outburst before calling his subject "socially primitive, sadly suspicious and forever the man-child."

One exception in the media was another *Sports Illustrated* writer, Barbara La Fontaine. Watching as reporters baited him with questions about his birth date, which no one believed was really May 1932, La Fontaine responded with the voice she seemed to wish her subject could muster. She called her fellow reporters "curiously spiteful [in an] effeminate way; the word for it would be catty—if catty were strong enough."

A fictional birth date might have seemed like the least of Sonny's troubles. But, as La Fontaine sensed, it created a vacuum that he could never fill. A man without a birth certificate is missing something everyone else takes for granted: a reference point. Not having one made Sonny feel like an afterthought, lacking even a census record to document his arrival.

But instead of being allowed to deal with it privately, the press forced to him defend himself against an obvious lie. As one of the few reporters who was able to get close to Sonny, Jack McKinney of the *Philadelphia Daily News*, later put it: "When guys wrote that he was 32 going on 50, it had more of an impact than anybody realized. Sonny didn't know who he was. He was looking for an identity and he thought being champion would give him one."

By the time he moved full-time to Vegas in 1966, Sonny was

done trying to rehabilitate himself. Let Floyd Patterson win all the humanitarian awards. Let Ali be the voice of his generation. Let those "educated" Negroes fuck themselves.

Sonny hadn't traveled all these miles to get into fights that weren't his own.

4.

SHADOW BOXING

On September 23, 1968, Ash Resnick drove his Ford LTD past the broad entrance of Caesars Palace, with its lines of cypress trees and the fountains that shot 10,000 gallons of water a minute into the air. Mondays were always busy days for casinos, because they had to tally action from the weekend. But this was going to be an especially trying Monday: Resnick had a meeting with the FBI.

One small but telling statistic revealed the permanent level of paranoia that had settled over Las Vegas: there were six hundred active wiretaps spread around the city. *Six hundred.* That was enough to plant twenty in every hotel. And Resnick would have been naive if he didn't think that at least one of those bugs was for him. He was a jowly, fast-talking Brooklyn native and everything that a wannabe in Las Vegas wanted to be, with a huge office that overlooked the Strip and a card file that included everyone who was anyone in sports. He also looked the part, with a belly that strained against his shiny suits and a neck that spilled over his collar when he chose to knot a tie. He'd been dealing with the FBI since he was a kid back east and played basketball for the Albany-Troy Celtics of the New York State Professional Basketball League. A photo in the Troy *Times Record* from 1947 captured the point guard crouching in the moment before he either passed the ball or broke someone's nose. With Resnick's tough-guy image, it was hard to tell.

In those days, the bookmaker spent his spare time at the racetrack taking bets in the bar. When the local cops tagged him as an undesirable and chased him out of town, he tried relocating to Florida before deciding to do what all the other mob-connected bookies were doing and make the migration to Las Vegas.

Initially, Resnick applied for a dealer's license at the Tropicana. But then he came to the attention of the Clark County Sheriff's Department after it got complaints that he was running an unauthorized sports book "out of his pocket" at the El Rancho Vegas hotel. The former basketball star—who by then had ballooned to well over 220 pounds—tried to claim that he was working as an athletic trainer. But deputies who found $1,456 in his pocket arrested him on vagrancy charges and placed him on a watch list that he was never quite removed from. An FBI report from that era linked him to the Genovese crime family figure Charlie "The Blade" Tourine.*

To stop exactly what Resnick had been accused of doing, Congress passed a law in 1961 that outlawed sending information about betting across state lines. But by then Resnick had already begun to soften his image to get away from the small-time-bookie label and surrounded himself with famous friends. "When I met Ash at Caesars I thought he was Caesar," says Gene Kilroy, then a close aide to Cassius Clay. "He could do whatever he wanted there. Everyone kissed his ring. If he put it in his back pocket, they'd kiss his ass." Caesars had more convention space than any hotel on the Strip, and when they poured into the casino after a long day, Resnick made sure his famous friends were there to pose for a photo or shake some hands so his guests had a lifetime memory to take back home.

The FBI, however, was concerned about more than photos. One of Resnick's closest friends in Las Vegas was Joe Louis, whom he had met while standing on line for his army physical in 1942. When Joe's free-spending ways started to catch up with him in the 1950s, Resnick was the one who invited him to Vegas and put him up in a bungalow. In one FBI debriefing, Louis was described as being "used by ASH now as bodyguard companion.

---

*A decade later, Resnick told the writer Pete Hamill that he'd spent the fifties vacationing in Lake Worth, Florida, at a hotel bungalow next door to one used by FBI director J. Edgar Hoover and his gay lover, Clyde Tolson. "I'd sit with [them] on the beach every day," Resnick said. "We were family." Resnick also claimed that Meyer Lansky neutralized Hoover in Vegas by obtaining erotic photos of Hoover and Tolson together. He referred to Lansky as the guy "who put everything together."

Stooge for casino. Shoots craps constantly. Ash supplies money. Golf and craps are only interests for Joe. . . . In discussions with Joe, believe he really dislikes Ash but has no other route—Ash treats him like royalty and will give him any money he asks for to gamble." Thanks to Resnick, Louis became one of the original investors in the Moulin Rouge and a greeter at Caesars. But what concerned the FBI was the way that Resnick had begun taking the beloved champ on collection calls that involved some not-so-thinly veiled threats. The FBI's Las Vegas office reported the woes of a gambler who lost $60,000 on dice at the casino and got a call from Resnick telling him that if he didn't pay up, "we have other means of getting the money."

The FBI was just as worried about Resnick's association with the NBA star Wilt Chamberlain. A memo dated February 1968, when the future Hall of Famer was playing in Philadelphia, detailed a suspicious episode in which the center announced after a lopsided loss in New York that he had a sore knee and probably wouldn't be playing the next night's game against the St. Louis Hawks on a neutral court in Miami. But when the 76ers arrived in Florida as heavy underdogs, Chamberlain's knee suddenly got better and he scored twenty-one points as he led Philadelphia to a 119–93 blowout. The FBI took a dim view of the fact that Resnick and Louis visited the 76ers locker room before the game and got free tickets to sit in the press box next to Frank Sinatra. The same source who told the Bureau about Louis said that when Chamberlain moved to Los Angeles to play for the Lakers, he was "Ash's guest at [Caesars Palace] almost every week-end date [the team] was at home or Phoenix." Chamberlain's association with Resnick was such a noxious open secret that many casinos wouldn't even list Lakers games.

But neither Louis nor Chamberlain was on the FBI's agenda this day. Sonny was.

Athan Theoharis, an FBI historian, notes that many of the pages in Liston's 129-page file bear the initials of top officials, indicating "he was being closely watched by the entire top rung of the agency." When Sonny's old antagonist, the U.S. senator from Tennessee, Estes Kefauver, rallied to his side by telling the press that he believed Sonny had finally "gotten rid of the tentacles of the underworld," Hoover scribbled on the report that was sent to him, "Just how naive can some of our VIPs get?"

Before Resnick could pull out chairs for the agents, they asked him if he'd be willing to sign a form waiving his rights to a lawyer. He glanced at the form and said sure. Why not? He didn't have anything to hide. Now, what was this all about, again?

The agents brought up the name of a veteran gambler, Barnett Magids, who'd been quietly feeding them information from a prison where he'd been sent for swindling banks in his native Houston.

Resnick often carried the air of a world-weary executive who was constantly being forced to answer for things that were out of his control, and he sighed when he heard the name. Yes, he said, he knew the real estate investor. Magids came to Vegas from Houston a lot in the early sixties when Resnick held the vague but important-sounding title of "sports director" at the Thunderbird, a squat bric-a-brac hotel on the Strip with a pair of huge

Navajo war birds in the parking lot. Magids became one of the hotel's high rollers, going as much as a hundred thousand dollars into debt.

Resnick knew that Magids held a grudge over a series of business deals. One involved twenty grand he'd lost in an insider stock opportunity. Feeling jilted, Magids flew to Vegas to get it back and found Resnick shooting craps with $20,000 in chips on the table. The two men had words and Resnick told Magids to wait for him in the lobby. An hour later, he came out pissed. As an FBI report on the incident noted, "Resnick claimed that Magids had jinxed him" and they were even on the twenty grand.

Magids had other stories, too, like the one about Resnick taking Joe Louis with him to Houston to settle a $7,500 debt from the Thunderbird. (Magids claimed Resnick pocketed the money and never settled the debt, leaving him to get hounded when the hotel got sold to new owners.) But the story that really caught the agents' attention was the one Magids told about Resnick's links to Liston.

Sonny had met Ash in 1963 when he came to Vegas to train for his second fight with Floyd Patterson and stayed at the Thunderbird. Resnick threw himself into the role of maître d'hôtel, offering Sonny everything from fine clothes to consorts to a few well-timed jackpots for Geraldine in his casino. He even turned himself into Sonny's de facto publicist, running a PR operation from the coffee shop with a phone permanently cradled in his ear from which he lured high rollers by promising them private viewings of the champ. Magids said he was one of them, claiming he was given "a big buildup to Liston."

Sonny's second demolition of Patterson paralleled Resnick's rise in the Liston camp. He joined Sonny when he traveled to Miami in 1964 to defend his title against Clay and rented the Listons an oceanfront mansion on the Intracoastal Waterway in Miami. (He also paid for a place on Collins Avenue where Sonny could go to meet prostitutes. As the boxing writer Jack McKinney later told *New Yorker* editor David Remnick, "That's what Ash Resnick brought him in the way of intellectual and cultural enrichment.") The night before the fight, he even put on Three Stooges movies to relax his fighter.

Because Ash had no official title in Liston's camp, the newcomer was viewed skeptically by the ones who did. It was one thing when he helped out at the Thunderbird. Everything turned out okay in Vegas. But when he flew to Miami, Sonny's regulars kept shooting one another suspicious looks, wondering what the hell the guy in fine cashmere suits was doing at their training camp. So was Florida's attorney general, who would mention a "well known gambler and bookmaker [who] enjoyed the full run of the training camp and was present in Liston's dressing room prior to the fight."

According to the story that Magids told the FBI, Resnick invited him to an all-expenses-paid vacation at the Fontainebleau Hotel to watch the fight as a kind of repayment for all the money he'd dropped in Vegas. Ultimately, Magids couldn't make the trip, but he said he did call Resnick there a few days beforehand. As he told the agents, "Resnick said that Liston would knock Clay out in the second round" but that he should wait until the day of the fight to place his bets "because the odds may come down."

Magids thanked him and took the advice. A few hours before fight time, he called Resnick again. This time, according to the FBI report, Resnick urgently told him to forget everything they'd spoken about and "not make any bets but just go watch the fight on pay TV." Resnick hurried off the phone, insisting he couldn't say more.

Considering that the pre-fight odds were 7–1 in Sonny's favor, it was odd advice. Most experts agreed with Sonny that Clay was too flighty to fight at a championship level. He'd made the trip to Miami in February 1964 in the same rickety bus that he'd driven to Denver a few months earlier and pulled up to the Listons' home. It was past midnight and Sonny's neighbors in the white suburb were not amused to see a black man poking a flashlight in windows and blaring the horn in an attempt to get a rise out of the champ. Seven police cruisers and a K-9 unit were called to dispatch Clay.

Clay continued his antics all the way to the pre-fight weigh-in in Miami. In a ballroom full of reporters from seventeen countries, he went on a bizarre tirade that won him a $2,500 fine from the Miami Beach Boxing Commission for screaming, "This is my show!" At ten the next night, February 25, Magids tuned in to see the bout on a feed supplied by Theater Network Television, a company that hired Joe Louis to do color commentary and was charging $4 to $10 so fans could watch in one of 350 theaters as well as a small but growing market of in-home pay TV networks. (Thanks to the fact that the start time was ten o'clock on a Tuesday night and the top ticket price was $250, the Miami Beach Convention Center was only half full.)

Sonny's entrance was slow and deliberate. Dressed in a white terry-cloth robe that advertised Resnick's Thunderbird Hotel, he took his time getting to the ring, where Clay was already bouncing nervously. Once Sonny slipped through the ropes, he kept his back to the challenger while Clay held out his gloves so one of Sonny's cornermen could inspect them.

It was the last moment of supplication Clay would allow. At the opening bell, Clay briefly played into the concerns about his foolishness by carrying his arms dangerously low. But then he slipped the first half-dozen of Sonny's punches with surprising speed and used a 180-degree flurry of jabs to launch into his own brutal combination. Sonny rallied in the second, but by the third round it was clear to Magids why Resnick told him to pull his money. There was not going to be an early knockout on this night.

At the end of the fourth round, there was a bizarre moment in which Clay's eyes started to burn and he flailed around his corner, sure he was going blind. The cause of the burning was probably liniment oil, though where it came from was the subject of great debate. It could have accidentally dripped into Clay's eyes from one of the towels that his trainers were using, or, if it came from Sonny's gloves, as Clay's camp suspected, it could have been the result of accidental spillage and not a dirty trick. Nonetheless, Clay panicked and almost didn't come out to face the fifth.

As the writer Rob Sneddon noted in his 2015 book *The Phantom Punch: The Story Behind Boxing's Most Controversial Bout*, Clay was wildly paranoid about being sabotaged, because of the growing influence of the Nation of Islam on him. Malcolm X, the Nation's charismatic spokesman, spent most of the month of February with Clay in Miami, instructing him on why he should distrust white people. Clay, who was on the verge of changing his name to Muhammad Ali, became so jittery that he wouldn't even let his doctor touch his water bottle for fear someone might slip something into it. In his corner, Clay kept screaming, "Stop it! Stop it!" which his trainer, Angelo Dundee, feared meant he wanted the fight stopped.

"He said, 'Cut the gloves off. I want to prove to the world there's dirty work afoot,'" Dundee later recalled in a television interview. "And I said, 'Whoa, whoa, back up, baby. C'mon now, this is for the title, this is the big apple. What are you doing? Sit down!' So I get him down, I get the sponge and I pour the water into his eyes trying to cleanse whatever's there, but before I did that I put my pinkie in his eye and I put it into my eye. It burned like hell. There was something caustic in both eyes."

Dundee single-handedly changed the course of both fighters' careers by forcing Clay to fight the fifth round. And by the time Clay's eyes cleared, he could tell that Sonny was winded. A case can be made that the fight should never have been held. Sonny had hurt his shoulder while training and needed cortisone treatments for bursitis in both shoulders the day before the bout. That no doubt accounted for Resnick's frantic advice to Magids hours before the fight to hold on to his money. And as the sixth round ended, Magids was grateful for the tip. After the furious pounding he gave Clay, Sonny could barely raise his left arm.

A lot of gamblers who took the sure bet on Sonny got wiped

out when his manager, Jack Nilon, stopped the fight. And, strangely, Resnick claimed he was among them. He told *Sports Illustrated* he'd lost his shirt on the travesty. But that made no sense to Magids. Why would Resnick squander his own money when he was telling others to hold on to theirs? Magids suspected that Resnick—knowing what he knew about Sonny's sore shoulders—bet the long odds on Ali and made himself a boatload of money. As he told the agents, "Resnick knew that Liston was going to lose."

A rematch was set for the Boston Garden nine months later, on November 16, 1964. There was so little appetite to see the two men face off that all twenty-nine state athletic commissions in the World Boxing Association refused to sanction the fight. Nevertheless, Sonny had cut himself down to his muscular essence, lean around the hips and neck. He started in Colorado, spending his mornings running at the Mother Cabrini Shrine in the mountains near Golden, where a statue of the Sacred Heart of Jesus stood atop a 373-step climb. Then he moved his camp to a WASPy country club in Plymouth, Massachusetts. Reporters were impressed when they saw Sonny taking his five-mile runs through the dunes, and Resnick arranged an unexpected show for a small group of journalists on the Friday before the fight. The 13–10 odds in Sonny's favor reflected the consensus that he'd rediscovered his murderous left jab. Even Clay's trainer, Angelo Dundee, admitted that being hit with his jab "was like getting hit with a telephone pole."

Clay didn't appear at that workout. He wanted to drop a sack of black cats on Liston as a Friday-the-thirteenth prank but thought twice. Instead, he settled down to a dinner of well-cooked steak, potatoes, and spinach at his hotel and picked the Edward G. Robinson gangster movie *Little Caesar* to take his mind off boxing. Halfway through the film, though, he started to feel nauseated and began vomiting. "Oh, something awful is wrong," he told his brother, Rudolph. Boston police were called to whisk Clay to City Hospital, where he was rushed into surgery for what turned out to be a herniated intestine, leading to an indefinite delay in the fight.

At that moment in Boston, Sonny Liston may have still believed he could control his destiny by winning back his title. But in some sad and ironic way, the sportswriters who saw him as Ash Resnick's puppet had a point. Even though he had the biggest fists in the history of boxing, his fate would always be in someone else's hands. And it was about to get passed among the politicians of Massachusetts.

In January 1965, Endicott Peabody, the state's Democratic governor and an enthusiastic backer of the fight, was replaced by a Republican who was far less enamored with big-time boxing. It's unclear if the new governor, John Volpe, communicated his displeasure to the Suffolk County district attorney, Garrett Byrne. But by April, as author Rob Sneddon points out, Byrne had become an outspoken opponent of the rescheduled fight, and Sonny didn't help by getting arrested for drunk driving in Denver. Byrne filed an injunction to stop the fight on the grounds that Sonny's Intercontinental Promotions had failed to apply for a license to do business in Massachusetts.*

Once a superior court judge agreed to hear arguments on the case in early May, the fight's backers decided to pull out of Boston and accept an offer from a promoter in Maine to use a youth center with fifty thousand seats that was two hours away, in Lewiston, Maine, a town of forty-one thousand residents.

Six hundred reporters descended on Lewiston to cover the rematch on May 25, making the textile town look like an advance station for an army base. Radio towers were hastily erected to beam the fight as far away as the USSR, and members of the local college track team were hired as couriers.

Although Sonny said that he expected an early decision, most boxing pros believed the fight would go to eight rounds. Their news-side colleagues and 240 police officers were on hand, meanwhile, for another reason: three months earlier, Malcolm X had been assassinated after growing disillusioned with the Nation of Islam, and there was grave talk that his supporters, who blamed the Nation for his death, had hired a hit squad to kill Ali as retaliation. (Fred Brooks, the head of the closed-circuit-TV company that was airing the fight, added to the theater by taking a $1 million life insurance policy out on Ali.)

---

* In *The Phantom Punch*, Sneddon argues that pressure might have also come from the Kennedy family. Jack Kennedy famously backed Patterson over Liston when he was president, and during his tenure as attorney general Robert Kennedy prosecuted Frank Carbo and Blinky Palermo, Liston's biggest mob backers. As Sneddon notes, Ted Kennedy, then in his first term in the Senate, might have felt freer to advance his brothers' anti-Liston agenda once Peabody left office.

To judge from the weigh-in, the crowd was on Sonny's side. He entered the arena in a white silk robe and flanked by his trainers, Willie Reddish and Teddy King, to cheers, while Ali arrived to taunts. "You'd better bring your pillow, Clay," one fan yelled. "Who is the greatest?" Ali shot back. "Sonny Liston?"

When the bell finally clanged later that night, Ali started strong, making a beeline to Sonny and introducing a hard right before he backpedaled so Sonny was forced to lunge into his punches. Sonny regained his footing with a bounce in his knees and started flicking his long jabs into Ali's body. But two minutes into the first round Ali maneuvered away from one of those jabs by lifting his right arm over the punch and bringing it squarely onto Sonny's cheekbone. The referee, Jersey Joe Walcott, would call it "one of the most devastating punches I've ever seen."

From the cheap seats, it looked glancing at best, a quick flick of Ali's glove that shouldn't have toppled a junior hockey player. A knot of students from Bates College started the chant of "Fix, fix, fix." And Sonny's reaction caused others in the audience to join them. Having fallen to his back, he woozily extended his arms behind him, then unsteadily staggered to his knee before he tipped back again and assumed the same supine position, as if it had been rehearsed. The rules dictated that Ali return to a neutral corner so the timekeeper could begin his count, but instead Ali stood over Sonny, yelling, "Get up and fight, sucker!"

Without realizing that the count had already begun, Walcott let Sonny climb back to his feet and the fight appeared to be ready to resume, when *The Ring*'s publisher, Nat Fleischer, yelled to Walcott that the timekeeper had reached twelve. As Walcott, who doubled as a cop in Camden, New Jersey, would later explain, "I was trying to pick up the count but I couldn't hear it. They should have had a loudspeaker. But I thought it was more important to keep that wild man Clay away from Liston than run over to get the count."

Once Walcott raised Ali's arms, observers were split on what they'd seen. Writing in *The New York Times*, Red Smith labeled Ali's winning shot a "phantom punch," while Tex Maule told *Sports Illustrated* readers, "It was a perfectly valid, stunning right-hand punch to the side of the head, and [Ali] won without benefit of a fix." Jimmy Breslin called the whole thing "the worst mess in the history of sports."

Politicians and pundits, meanwhile, chewed it over in loftier terms, decrying it as another slap at the fading social order. Cynicism might be having its day, but the boxing ring was the one place where old-fashioned values still mattered. Reporting on a sudden groundswell in Congress to ban prize fighting, the *Los Angeles Times* screamed: "IT ONLY TAKES MINUTE TO KILL BOXING."

Joe Louis, who was sitting at ringside, got his college-age son tickets for the bout and the two met up afterward to visit Sonny in his locker room. Considering the abrupt way Sonny had hit the canvas, Joe Jr. expected to see him receiving some kind of medical aid. "We were perplexed," he told me. "Because Sonny didn't seem to be hurt at all."

One of the most enduring explanations for what happened in Lewiston became known as the "secret percent theory." The details vary from telling to telling, but the basics involve someone in Sonny's camp, possibly Ash Resnick, meeting in secret with Ali's Nation of Islam managers to float some kind of proposal.

Sonny wasn't in the same shape as he'd been in before the Boston fight. All the energy and passion he'd built up—all the hate—seemed to have drained away. He spent his nights at a malt shop, laughing with the kids behind the soda fountain. Is it so strange to imagine him offering to take a dive in exchange for a cut of Ali's future earnings?

Such future-earnings deals weren't uncommon in boxing. When James Braddock agreed to meet Louis in 1937 at Chicago's Comiskey Park, their contract included an above-the-table provision for Braddock to get a cut of Louis's purses for a period thereafter—a shrewd move, since Louis won. And an under-the-table deal was precisely the kind of high-risk, high-reward gambit that Ash Resnick was a master at making.

There would also have been a certain amount of logic in such a deal for the Nation of Islam. Ali was its most public face and its best recruiting tool. A proposal to cut Sonny in on Ali's future earnings might have been seen as a reasonable opportunity cost—a modest investment to keep the Nation's recruitment machine greased and Ali on top. (No one at the time anticipated Ali's future draft troubles or the fact he was going to lose three of the most productive earning years of his life.)

Ali appeared to hint at some hidden machination when he told reporters a day before the fight, "It's gonna be a shock. If I were to predict what was to happen, no one would come to see the fight. That's how shocking it will be. They might even say the fight was fixed."

Ali may simply have been running his mouth, but the appearance of Ash Resnick at Sonny's side during the weigh-in left open the question. It didn't help that he was palling around Lewiston with Sam Margolis, the notorious Philadelphia deli owner who was widely considered a front for the mob.

Gene Kilroy, who was helping Ali handle his business affairs at the time, dismisses the idea that Resnick could have gotten close enough to the Nation of Islam to do a deal. "That's all bullshit," he told me. "There's no way that Elijah Muhammad would have gotten involved with anything like that, or even hold a conversation with Ash Resnick. I knew Elijah very well. He was very honorable. There's no chance that happened, at all."

Still, the theory endures, and one reason is that it presents Sonny as still being in control of his fate. Having been raised by Mafia opportunists, he would have understood the sense in letting Ali take the punishment from that point forward while he sat back and cashed the checks. Indeed, instead of seeing a dive as a surrender, he might have seen it as the most intelligent thing he could do.

It's a hopeful scenario, because the alternative is almost too cruel to consider: that Sonny was done in by an unbearable, even existential, dose of bad luck.

Almost immediately after Sonny hit the canvas in Lewiston, a race broke out among state athletic commissions to see who could punish him the fastest. When the dust settled, he was banned in so many places that he was literally a boxer without a country.

That made the mid-sixties difficult years for the Listons as they struggled to make ends meet. But those were also, in their own way, tranquil years. Sonny traveled to the beautiful Swedish port city of Gothenburg to barnstorm for ten grand a fight. "I'm staging my comeback campaign in Sweden because it seems impossible for me to get fights in my own country," Sonny told reporters.

He also came face-to-face with a child he never knew he had, when a twenty-seven-year-old waitress arrived at his hotel with a caramel-skinned boy who she announced was his son. Geraldine couldn't have been surprised that Sonny had cheated on her on one of his earlier visits. But there was something in the three-year-old boy that seemed to melt her anger away when she met him in June of 1966.

Geraldine had two daughters of her own, both born before she married Sonny. The Listons rarely discussed the girls in interviews, and the only widely published photo of them was a publicity still taken in 1964, before Sonny's first fight with Ali, when the girls were posed reading a mock children's book titled *How to Whup a Big Mouth*. They briefly lived with the Listons in Denver but there's little evidence they had much of a relationship with their stepfather, or even saw their mother regularly, by 1966, when Arletha would have been about twenty-one and Eleanor fifteen. All of which could explain why Geraldine was so taken by the boy. He offered her a chance to have the family with Sonny that she'd always wanted.

Everyone was discreet about the arrangements that were sub-sequently worked out. In an interview with Reuters, the Listons claimed that they'd met the waitress, Agnete Weise, while din-ing at their hotel and became taken with her. "Mr. and Mrs. Liston are wonderful people," Weise told the wire service. "I cannot give my son the home he deserves and Daniel, my boy, is getting the chance of his life. There will be no more staying at day schools for him while I am at work. I miss him, but I am happy he is with the Listons." In a final thought, she added: "Nobody can look after children the way Negroes can."

After the Listons returned to Las Vegas with Daniel in the spring of 1967, the *Chicago Tribune* dropped by Ottawa Drive to find the boy scampering around their "immaculate living room" and a backyard pool that "shimmered in the dazzling desert sun." Geraldine came off as detached about her husband's busi-ness affairs even as she subtly lobbied for his return. "Every-body's always hollering about the elements behind Charles," she told the paper, obliquely referring to his mob associations with Frank "Blinky" Palermo, among others. "But if that were true, he would have money. He's got enough to live. The trouble is, you've got to have some coming in, too, and we don't."

On a separate visit, *Sports Illustrated* also found that Sonny had mellowed. The magazine described him driving a big green Caddy along the Strip, lounging in health club saunas, and yell-ing, "Don't run out of gas, kid," as he watched the weekly Wednesday-night fights at the Silver Slipper. He was living what the article described as "the life of a country squire."

It was an upbeat portrayal. But it also contained a quote from a source described as a "Las Vegas gambling figure and Liston confidant" who sounded a note of caution. "The trouble is Sonny's got no money to put up," said the source, who with that description could easily have been Ash Resnick.

"He talks about buying into one of the hotels in Vegas, but what with? He has some money coming from his fights, money that was tied up, but he may never see any of that. When he went to Sweden to fight the first time, he had to borrow $3,000 from the bank on his car. He doesn't spend much. He doesn't throw it around. But remember: he was cut up pretty good. He never knew what was going on."

With Ash now having moved on to other things, Sonny drove to the Sands casino for a lunch with Sammy Davis Jr. in early 1968. The Rat Pack entertainer was trying to get into boxing and decided that promoting a Liston comeback was a fine place to start. Ed Sullivan, who was serving as a kind of advisor, was in the corner booth with him, as was Henry Winston, the only established black promoter in boxing. Everyone had the same thought: it was time for Sonny to get back to business.

If his jab had started to lose just a bit of its finishing power, those present all knew it was still plenty valuable. Staring at Sammy, Sullivan brought up the elephant in the room: "How do you propose getting around the questions that are going to be asked about organized crime?"

"Geraldine and Sonny were at a point in their lives where they needed and deserved a nest egg," Winston would tell me decades later. "But they couldn't make money without the Mafia guys putting their requests in." Sammy waved off the issue as irrelevant. "Don't worry about the mob," he told Sullivan in what appeared to be a thinly veiled reference to Resnick and his friends. "I've got control over them."

Winston was impressed. Figuring it was worth at least taking a chance, he agreed to use his contacts to see if he could get Sonny a fight license in California. Over the next couple of weeks, he began taking acquaintances on the California State Athletic Commission to expensive dinners to remind them that nothing had emerged from all the investigations into Sonny. Boxing was an unpredictable business. Sometimes one punch was all it took. Surely they could see that was what had happened in Lewiston. Surely it was time to let the man earn a living with what little time he had left.

Thanks to those expensive dinners, and perhaps a little extra dessert, the resistance to Sonny melted away. The difference between May 1965 and January 1968 in politics was an eternity. What seemed important in 1965 suddenly didn't seem so important now, and the commission formally announced that it was putting the issue of a fight license for Sonny on its end-of-the-month docket.

There was little doubt that Sonny was still a physical specimen. But the commission required a blood test. So, before the meeting, Winston brought him to his doctor in Oakland. The promoter was amazed when a nurse approached Sonny with a needle and the blood drained from his face as if he'd seen a ghost.

"He almost jumped in the nurse's lap," Winston recalled. "He wouldn't take the test that morning, so we had to go out and get lunch. All the time he was going crazy on me, 'Motherfucker' this, 'Motherfucker' that. It took a lot of work, but he finally gave the blood. That's how much he hated needles."

As expected at the commission's hearing in late January of 1968, Winston got pressed on whether Sonny had finally excised himself from the web of mobsters who had followed him since his days in St. Louis. Assuring them he had, Winston dropped Davis's name and vowed that both of them would do everything in their power to keep Sonny away from organized crime. When it came time for Sonny to speak, he kept it short and sweet. "I feel I've paid my debt to society and severed my ties with the underworld," he said.

On February 3, 1968, the commission approved his application.

While Barnett Magids continued to inform on Resnick to the FBI, Sonny started his comeback in Reno in March of 1968 against Bill McMurray, a California truck driver. There were no packs of people paying to see Sonny jump rope to "Night Train" this time around—and, tellingly, no Ash.

One of the few reporters to make the trip was the *New York Times* columnist Robert Lipsyte, who'd been at ringside for the second Ali fight. He was curious to see if Liston had anything left and found that little had changed in the three years since Lewiston. When he walked into the gym, Sonny was giving a hard time to a female photographer who was trying to shoot him for a local newspaper.

"There gotta be plenty of pictures of me. Use some of them," he barked. When the woman replied that she wanted "special" pictures, Sonny started backing her against the wall. "Special pictures?" he said, his voice rising. "What do you want me to do? You want me to take my shirt off? How do you want me to pose?" He continued until her small frame was entirely covered by his shadow.

"If you don't want me to take any photos, that's fine," she said, standing her ground. "There won't be any in our paper. But I don't have to take this shit." Lipsyte waited for Sonny to erupt, but instead he broke into a broad grin and gave her all the time she needed.

Maybe he had softened after all.

The comeback camp had a celebratory feel, with the rock group the Monkees hanging out beside Sammy's PR man, Bill Rowe. Even Geraldine made the trip. But Sonny was ten pounds overweight, and when the opening bell rang, his lack of fitness showed. He came out slow and missed several chances to cash in on McMurray's missteps. It took Sonny four rounds to finally use his jab to end the fight.

Afterward, when Sonny proclaimed, "Joe Frazier will win the title and I'll beat him," Lipsyte began his column, "Another threat to the national sanity was posed last night when Sonny Liston punched Bill McMurray through the ropes and announced himself a candidate for the heavyweight championship of the world."

Sonny's next fight was at the Grand Olympic Auditorium in L.A., where the local promoter, Don Chargin, was happy to join in the comeback frenzy. The Reno fight had been poorly attended because of a snowstorm, but Chargin figured to sell seven or eight thousand tickets on Sonny's name. At first he got a little nervous when Sonny asked for an advance. That was always a sign that a fighter was hard up and unpredictable. But to Chargin's relief, he did every bit of press that was asked and proved altogether agreeable about it.

The bout against Billy "Willie Swift" Joiner, a slick boxer from Cincinnati who didn't have much punch, was a dreary affair. It took Sonny six rounds to finally put Joiner and himself out of their misery, and fans pelted the ring with garbage, shouting, "Go back to the Missouri state pen!"

But as 1968 wore on, it became harder to call Liston's comeback campaign quixotic. He took what *The Washington Post* called a "convincing win" in July by scoring a seventh-round TKO against the far younger Henry Clark in San Francisco. A few months later, in Phoenix, he stopped an ex–Dallas cop named Sonny Moore in the third. Before Thanksgiving, he embarrassed the unranked Roger Rischer at a benefit in Pittsburgh. And in a closed-circuit broadcast from Baltimore, he derailed one of his old sparring partners, Amos "Big Train" Lincoln.

He was back, back in the game. And it felt great. No, better than great! Lem Banker, a wealthy Vegas gambler who owned the Sahara Health Club and liked to hang around boxers, hit the trail with Sonny, putting them up in high-priced suites and paving the way for them to gorge on women.

It was more than just the road pussy, though. The Harlem snobs who had reviled Sonny back in the day were moving on to bigger battles. The reporters who were around him now were nicer, the fans were pulling for him, and, hell, even the cops were respectful. Sonny had come out the other side of the sixties as a genuine icon, and he even dressed like it, going out in slick shades, mock turtlenecks, and shiny pants.

It was still a little early for irony. That would come later, in the seventies. But it was ironic that the barefoot kid from Arkansas who came to America's attention wearing fedoras and wool coats would become an early exemplar of black gangster chic.

In Los Angeles, the bartender at the Beverly Wilshire hotel knew how to fix his vodkas just the way he liked them, on the rocks, and the studio executives at Paramount were suddenly interested in him for bit parts on TV shows. Interestingly, for someone who was viewed as scarily humorless, he surrounded himself with a rat pack that included such popular black comedians as Godfrey Cambridge, Nipsey Russell, and Redd Foxx.

There were still skeptics of Sonny, though.

In the not-for-attribution interview with *Sports Illustrated*, the source who sounded like Ash Resnick asked, "What will happen if Sonny's comeback fails?" He answered his own question by saying, "He'll go to work. Just plain take a job. Sonny's not proud. If he has to work in construction or something like that, why, that's exactly what he'll do."

But Sonny *was* proud. Too proud to let anyone think he'd gone down or out. During a lull in his fight schedule, he was hanging out at the Town Tavern when a local drunk started going on about what he'd just read in *Sports Illustrated*.

Sonny's friend Clyde Watkins was standing beside him, and as Watkins would remember it, the veins on Sonny's forehead began to pulse. After all that had transpired, Sonny was still sensitive to the claim that he was too dim to manage his own money. Wheeling around, he yelled, "I'll show you how broke I am!"

With his Cadillac still parked outside, Sonny threw Watkins into the driver's seat and ordered him to speed through red lights to his house on Ottawa Drive. While Watkins stood in the living room, Sonny ran up the stairs to his bedroom and started banging and clanging. Ten minutes later, he emerged with two thousand dollars in a pillowcase.

Still in a fever, he threw Watkins back in the car and had him speed right back to the Town Tavern, where he emptied the money in stacks all over a blackjack table. Then he stared down anyone who dared meet his eyes.

"That's how broke I am, motherfuckers."

The FBI agents in Ash Resnick's office scribbled notes on their thin pads, taking down his denials in detail.

Fix a fight? *Come on, boys.* Anyone who'd been around Sonny in Miami knew he was taking Clay lightly. He had alcohol on his breath and seemed unfocused. If he didn't get an early knockout, the odds were good he was going to have trouble in the later rounds.

Resnick also denied that he'd taken two checks from Magids worth $50,000 to place illegal bets on football games while he was the sports director at the Thunderbird. As far as he was concerned, the bigger question was why the FBI was trusting a swindler like Magids. The man was destitute, his family had abandoned him, and he was manic-depressive to boot. (An agent who interviewed him in prison noted that Magids "SHOULD BE CONSIDERED AS HAVING SUICIDAL TENDEN-CIES.") Resnick understood that the FBI had to do its job. But surely they had better ways of wasting his time than with a story like this from a guy looking to get out of a ten-year prison sentence.

The feds thanked him and got up to leave.

Upon returning to their office, the agents typed up the notes from the interview and forwarded them to their superiors in Washington.

What they hadn't mentioned to Resnick was that Magids had suddenly gotten cold feet about testifying against him in court. "He stated he knows what kind of people these are and how they operate," an agent who interviewed Magids noted four days earlier. "And he is fearful of what they might do to his wife and family if he testified—especially while he is still serving time."

On the last day of 1968, a high-ranking Justice Department lawyer typed out a memorandum that concluded, "There is not sufficient evidence obtained to justify seeking an indictment in this matter," meaning that, for the moment, Resnick was in the clear.

But the casino boss understood that J. Edgar Hoover wasn't going to stop digging into his past. Sonny and Ash had been done with each other for three years. But those two Ali fights weren't going away. Another memo sent directly to Hoover concluded that Resnick was "the fix point of [the] two heavyweight title fights. He had always been and will continue to be a corruption source for professional sports until he is stopped."

You couldn't get any blunter than that.

Resnick had traveled a long way since his days taking bets at the New York racetracks. He loved his house in Paradise Palms, his beautiful showgirl wife, the respect that came from having a big office in a lavish resort like Caesars. If the FBI wanted to take those things away from him, they'd have to pry them out of his white-knuckled hands.

And if Sonny ever tried to help them . . .

5.

HEROIN HEIGHTS

W"here are we going?"

"Take a left," the passenger said, directing Sonny.

Sonny took the left and cruised until he arrived at the front of a flat beige single ranch home in Charleston Heights, a subdivision of Las Vegas that catered to working families and temporary casino help.

Sonny's passenger was Mark Rodney, a long-haired teenager who wouldn't normally have had anything to do with a fifty-year-old ex–heavyweight champion, except that his father ran one of the most successful criminal crews in the city.

"How much?" Sonny said.

Mark checked his notepad. According to what his father told

him, they were about to knock on the door of a dentist who'd been hitting his nitrous oxide a little too hard and moved on to heroin.

"It says here five hundred."

The amount made Sonny run a certain calculation in his head. He reached down to his ankle for the .38 he kept strapped there and made sure it was loaded. "Okay, five hundred," he said.

He got out and took a look around. It was that time of day in Vegas when everyone either was going to bed after an overnight shift or was already out of the house for the morning, which meant there wouldn't be anyone to give them any trouble. For the most part, their customers were high-functioning junkies who paid on time, which was the way Sonny liked it. He didn't need to be messing with the strung-out pimps he ran into on trips through the Westside.

Mark's father also split the work so that another of his crews did the drops. Mark was purely on the collections side, which had the dual benefit of keeping him away from the drugs and letting him keep an eye on the family's money. Sonny was there for muscle.

The man who answered the door looked like he didn't belong near anyone's mouth. Sonny, for all of his bad habits, had perfect teeth—something he owed to his genetics and not letting anyone get near his face when he fought. (By contrast, he used to punch so hard that his sparring partners ended their sessions by picking teeth out of their mouth guards.) The dentist's teeth had a yellow glaze over them. A couple of them might have even been loose.

"Did we wake you?" Sonny asked.

"No, uh, uh, no . . ." the dentist said.

"We're here for what you owe," he said.

"Yeah, sure, sure," the dentist said, and disappeared back into his house.

Mark and Sonny exchanged glances, knowing what was coming.

When the dentist appeared a minute later, Sonny jammed his leather shoe into the door, just to be on the safe side.

"Um, there's a little problem," he said.

Mark looked to Sonny, whose expression didn't change. "We don't really do problems, man," he said.*

The dentist handed over a crumpled roll. "Here's a hundred and fifty," he said. "I'll get you the rest tomorrow. I promise."

Mark once again looked at Sonny. The great thing about working with the Champ was that it never took much. A twitch of his eye. A slight flex of his fist. Maybe just a little flare in his nostrils. For such a badass, he could be remarkably subtle. This time he adjusted his perfectly creased pants enough to lift his leg and reveal the loaded .38.

"Really, I don't have it all," the dentist said, pleading. He went back into the house and came up with a hundred more.

Mark counted the money, made a note in his pad, and said, "Okay, but no deliveries until we have the rest."

---

*Or something like that. In an interview four decades later, Rodney did the best he could with the memory.

Back in the car, Sonny shook his head in disgust. "Shit, did you see what those teeth looked like? That must be some ugly pussy he's eating."

This was late 1969, and Sony's comeback was pointing to one place.

Joe Frazier was on the kind of roll Sonny could only dream about. He'd just been on the *Today* show and had his pick of fights. The one he claimed not to care about was the one everyone was clamoring for: a showdown with Muhammad Ali.

As past his prime as Sonny now was, he still had a fighter's conviction that, if not for some bad luck, he'd be climbing into the ring against the new champ first. Instead, he was using his fists to make collections.

Later that night, when Sonny returned to Rodney's home and explained to Mark's father why they were short, the old man gave them a disapproving look. "He's got the money," he said. "The fucker has a safe with about twenty grand in jewelry in it."

R obert Chudnick was a legendary jazz trumpeter who also went by the stage name Red Rodney and led the kind of double life that could only flourish in a place like Las Vegas. He'd hop a flight to Burbank to play on *The Tonight Show Starring Johnny Carson* one night and be back in Vegas by nightfall selling heroin. So, in the seams of celebrity Las Vegas, it was inevitable that a jazz legend who loved boxing and a boxing legend who loved jazz would cross paths. Whether it was at the International, where they both worked, or at one of the parties thrown by friends like Sammy Davis Jr., Las Vegas was too small a town for them not to meet. And when they did, they understood that they were cut from the same cloth.

What Sonny admired most about Chudnick was that he was unreconstructed by his fame. To most of the world he was a genial trumpet player who lived in a spacious Spanish colonial on a block full of weeping palms. To those in the know, however, he was a compulsive thief who couldn't resist an easy score. And, like Sonny, he'd traveled far and wide, only to keep coming back to the same place.

The two men couldn't have started out any more differently. While Sonny was still working his father's peanut fields in Arkansas, Chudnick was growing up as a musical prodigy in a white Jewish home in Philadelphia, picking up jobs playing with the big bands. His life changed on the day when he went to the Downbeat Club in South Philly and watched Dizzy Gillespie. He was thunderstruck by the faster, improvisational music that Gillespie was pioneering. When Gillespie introduced him to Charlie Parker, his future was set.

Parker was impressed enough with Chudnick to invite the young trumpeter into his quintet, making him the only white musician to be part of the creation of bebop. But certain adjustments had to be made. When the band played in the racially segregated South, Chudnick pretended to be an albino so they wouldn't run afoul of public accommodation laws barring mixed-race bands. He got away with it because he had fiery red hair and a yellow-tinged skin color that was accentuated by his heroin use.

In those days, half the jazz world used the stuff. But there came a bottoming out in 1960, when Chudnick found himself destitute in San Francisco. Desperate for money, he swindled $10,000 by impersonating an army officer. By the time he was convicted and sentenced to twenty-seven months in prison, he was almost relieved. It gave him a chance to kick his habit and study some law while he was behind bars.

After being released, Chudnick moved to Las Vegas for yet another fresh start. There was plenty of musical work on the Strip, but as far as he was concerned, it was the soul-destroying kind. Every so often he'd get an invitation from Elvis or Ella or Streisand—artists he felt were worthy of his musical talents. But more often than not, he found himself gigging in second-tier lounges with the kind of corny crooners he once mocked. He became so depressed that after the shows he hit the strip clubs or casino bars and, before he knew it, the needles were coming out and he was going into the bathrooms to tie off and get back on the junk. It didn't take long for him to begin selling to his musician friends, too, and then to their friends.

Like all successful drug dealers, Chudnick was paranoid about his business. He took precautions like burying his drugs under garbage in his backyard at 4145 Gibraltar Street and splitting batches into tiny plastic pouches so that if a courier got caught he could swallow it and shit it out later. Mark and Sonny were recent additions to his crew. Mark had grown up with his mother in Hollywood Hills but yearned to live with his father. "He was so famous in the bebop era that he knew everybody, all the big musicians," Mark told me. "Every time he went to L.A.

he got invited on the Carson show to play with Doc [Severinsen] and the band. He knew Doc real well. He knew all those guys. We always fought about music: jazz versus rock. We were like cats and dogs. But I really wanted to join his crew, really bad. At the time, I thought it was cool."

Chudnick initially resisted the idea. Yet eventually he saw the wisdom in having a family member keep an eye on things. On a night when he was out to dinner with a wealthy friend, he gave his teenage son the blueprints to the friend's house along with a stolen key and told him where he would find a safe filled with cash and jewelry. "Don't fuck it up," he said. "You fuck it up, you're never going to do nothing for me."

He didn't fuck it up.

"There was a lot of shit my dad wouldn't tell me," Mark went on. "Like, I'd get a call from him: 'Go in my closet in the back room and do that thing I told you about,' which meant he wanted me to get the shovel he kept in the closet and bury the drugs we were keeping in the house in the backyard. I had to do that a bunch of times so there wasn't anything in the house. There was all kinds of shit."

Mark met Sonny for the first time at a party that his father took him to at 2058 Ottawa Drive. It was one of the shindigs that Sonny threw when Geraldine wasn't around, which was becoming more frequent by late 1969. Entertainment types like the actress Barbara McNair and the outlandish R&B performer Wayne Cochran chatted with Sonny's friends from the gyms, and strippers were draped over every piece of open furniture. Chudnick warned his son that Sonny could be mean and standoffish, but somehow the two made a connection, perhaps because Mark was still in his teens and Sonny always loved kids.

"I hear you like rock-and-roll music," Sonny said, handing him a copy of the *Sgt. Pepper* album cover.

"Groovy. Can you sign it for me?" Mark asked. That was when he saw the side of Sonny that his dad warned him about. The big man glowered and turned away. It was only later, when Mark asked his father what he'd done wrong, that he learned Sonny never gave autographs because he was embarrassed about not being able to sign his own name very well.

"When I . . . saw him the first few times, he was a happy guy," Mark recalled. "He was smiling all the time. My dad would be, like, 'Hey there, Sonny boy!' It got dirty later. Drugs always do that to every relationship. But I used to joke around with him and he'd smile because he knew I wasn't making fun."

The Chudnick home on Gibraltar Street became a refuge for Sonny. "In the beginning he used to come around a lot," Mark continued. "We had a music studio and if I wasn't in there, my dad would go in there with his friends. Sonny was sniffing a lot of heroin. I knew he was doing heroin up there because I did it with Sonny, too. He wasn't going to do heroin in front of his boxing friends. But my dad was a musician junkie and so was I, then. We were in the dope and the crime and the money business. [Sonny] could do stuff around us that he couldn't do with anyone else. That's why he liked hanging around us."

Sonny eventually became a full-fledged member of their crew and Mark's travel partner. The two would spend their business hours going door-to-door in places like Charleston Heights, which they nicknamed Heroin Heights. Sometimes after work, Sonny and Mark would go out for a drink, and one night Sonny took Mark to a bar he knew on the north end of Las Vegas Boulevard. Instead of inviting him in, however, he told his teenage sidekick to wait in the car.

As Mark waited and waited, he kept his eye on the clock until he finally became nervous about sitting in a parked car in an all-black neighborhood with five thousand dollars in cash in his pocket. He knew his father would be eyeing the clock as well, furious at him for not coming straight home with the loot. So, against Sonny's express instructions, he got out and went into the bar.

Instantly, he regretted it. It was pitch-black and pulsating under the sound of soul music. He spotted Sonny at the bar, dealing in small aluminum foil wrappers that he guessed were packets of cocaine.

As Mark recalled it, "Everyone just stared at me, like, 'What the fuck is he doing here?' I was a hippie. I had long hair and shit. Sonny saw me and said, 'Oh, he's with me.' But he was mad. He didn't talk to me all the way home."

A t that point, the two top spots in the heavyweight division were the property of Joe Frazier and Jimmy Ellis,* both of whom were scheduled to meet at Madison Square Garden in

---

*After the WBA stripped Ali of his title, it held an eight-man elimination bout to find a successor, which Ellis won. Frazier boycotted the tournament in solidarity with Ali, earning a separate New York State title.

early 1970. Sonny and his new trainer, veteran fight man Dick Sadler, desperately wanted a piece of the winner, and Sadler lobbied a new sanctioning body known as the North American Boxing Federation to help. Supported by eight states, including Nevada, and run by the head of the California Athletic Commission, the NABF didn't have the cachet of the World Boxing Association. But it had an office near Sadler's gym and a title to give out, and that's all he needed.

Once Sonny ran his record to 49–3 after fighting again in May and September, the question was who would be the last piece of the comeback puzzle. In early November of 1969, Sadler approached him with the idea of Leotis Martin, a former sparring partner. Martin had a habit of planting himself in one place for long periods, which made him inconsistent and vulnerable to bad luck. He'd also been doing a lot of fighting lately, which meant he'd be tired and unlikely to last long against Sonny's jab.

ABC had an opening on its *Wide World of Sports* in a few weeks. Would he do it? Sure, Sonny said, and the wheels were set in motion. The Vegas oddsmakers liked Sonny so much that they had him as high as a 14–5 favorite, and the crowd in the 2,300-seat showroom of the International on December 6, 1969, was just as enthusiastic as it gave him a standing ovation. Scanning the ringside seats, Sonny saw Sammy Davis Jr. next to Ed Sullivan giving him two thumbs-up. Howard Cosell was there to make the call for ABC's *Wide World of Sports*.

But Sonny's high-stakes gambling friend, Lem Banker, had a queasy feeling about the fight. "He had a cold that morning, and

Geraldine didn't want him to go," he'd recall. "The whole thing happened too quick."

Martin prepared carefully, seeing all the things that Liston's camp took as negatives as positives. Sure, the ten pounds he gave away made him susceptible to Liston's jab, but it also made him quicker, and all the fighting he'd been doing gave him the confidence to know he could get knocked down and get up, especially since Sonny didn't have the punching power he once had.

On the day of the fight, it was a lean and confident-looking Sonny who walked into the showroom of the International, bobbing in his bathrobe as his hometown crowd cheered, "Come on, Sonny!" and "Looking good, champ." Martin, who had a scruffier look with his bushy black mustache and long sideburns, was more subdued. His plan was to stay out of Liston's reach as much as possible, then pull inside. But in the early rounds the fight went pretty much the way the oddsmakers expected. Sonny used his left jab to dictate the pace, slowing Martin down just enough to knock him off his feet in the fourth with a sweeping left hook. But to Sonny's surprise, Martin came back stronger, dancing faster and faster as the next rounds sped by. This was exactly the kind of fight Sadler didn't want to have, and his concern grew as Martin started landing jabs, bloodying Sonny's nose. By the start of the ninth round, Cosell sounded like he belonged on a police radio when he described the cut on Sonny's nose as "a brutal, ugly sight. He's virtually snorting blood."

Seeing that Martin's eyes were swollen, Sonny tried to close them with his jab. He pounded Martin three straight times. But instead of going down, Martin came back with a right cross, left hook, right cross combo that lifted the twenty-pound-heavier Liston off his feet. By the next morning Martin would wake up in the hospital with a detached retina that would end his career. But for the moment Sonny was the one who was out. By the time he opened his eyes, a ring doctor was standing over him with ammonia capsules.

It's hard to know how much he was able to process while he tried to shake the blurriness out of his eyes. But he managed to be remarkably poised in his post-fight interview with Cosell. "Will you continue your career or is it over?" the broadcaster asked.

"Well, it's hard to say," he replied.

"It'll be hard to go up the trail again."

"Yes, it would be," Sonny said, a weak smile playing across his lips. "I'll have to see."

As soon as he got home, Sonny threw down his things and walked quietly to his pool, where stared blankly ahead. He'd been in front on all three cards when he got knocked out: 37–34, 38–35, and 38–36. All he had to do was hang in a little longer. He was that close to getting that one more fight a boxer always wants, which in his case was a meeting with Joe Frazier. Now all anyone would remember was that he went out against a former sparring partner who would never fight again.

Geraldine had planned a post-fight party and it was too late to cancel it now. So Sonny stayed by the pool as guests filtered in to offer handshakes and conciliatory words. But as the evening wore on, she felt her husband's mood darken. George Foreman would recall that when he arrived, Geraldine finally decided that she'd had enough of all the long faces and exploded in front of her guests: "What you guys gotta understand is that sometimes you lose. You can't win them all. Nobody wins them all."

Then she turned to the younger heavyweight and said something that she hoped everyone, especially Sonny, would take to heart.

"You hear that, George? You lose. Everybody loses. But you can't just die!"

N early a year to the day that John Sleeper arrested Earl Cage in the operation that left Sonny narrowly avoiding being shot, the police lieutenant gathered his agents to tell them that they were heading into the sheriff's department's territory once again.

The men in the room looked at one another with a sense of adventure. Even in a town as colorful as Vegas, the sheriff of Clark County, Ralph Lamb, was in a league by himself. One of eleven children born to horse ranchers in the farming town of Alamo, the six-foot-five Lamb gravitated to police work early, while his older brother, Floyd, entered politics. He became a sheriff's deputy at the age of twenty-one and worked there until he decided to open his own private detective agency. (His main client was Howard Hughes.) Six years later, when the incumbent sheriff retired, the thirty-one-year-old Mormon ran for the seat and was handily elected.

Combining a cowboy image with a knack for public relations,

Lamb made an immediate impression on the city. He rousted the two-bit con men who lurked around the Greyhound station, making them think twice about tripping out-of-towners to steal their wallets and running other crude scams. He also made life miserable for mobsters who used Vegas to escape whatever cops were on their tails by enforcing an ordinance that required convicts to register as soon as they hit town. (It was that same ordinance that led Sonny to fill out the Convicted Persons Questionnaire when he arrived in Vegas in 1966.) As Gary Beckwith, a deputy who worked undercover for Lamb, would recall: "We had a blue binder book that had pictures of all the known career criminals and a short story on them and their associates. Whenever we saw somebody in that book, we found a way to take them to jail."

Lamb's power grew along with the Strip. Since it was unincorporated and lay outside the boundary of the Las Vegas PD, he was its top cop. And since he also sat on a commission that handed out liquor and gaming licenses, he influenced nearly every job there, too. When the Beatles arrived in 1964 to play the Convention Center, he demanded that they first make an appearance at his office to register as performers. After a street sweep nabbed seventy-four Hells Angels, Lamb made them get haircuts before he dismantled their bikes and released the bikers into the desert.

Sonny got his own taste of Lamb when he moved to town full-time in 1966. "Sonny lived out by the Stardust Golf Course, which was in county territory, and when he first came to town Ralph went out to visit him," H. Lee Barnes, a veteran of the department, told me. "He said right up front, 'Listen, you've beaten up a couple of cops in Denver. You're not going to beat up any of my cops or my officers'—'any of my *boys*' is probably the way he put it—'and if you do, you're only one and I've got more than a hundred of them.'

"So one day I pull off Eastern onto Ottawa Drive, just doing regular patrolling, and I see Sonny has this pink Cadillac that's stalled on the street. He can't get it to start and he's trying to push it. I get out and I help him push it and he doesn't even look at me. So I just stood there staring at him and said, 'Hey, asshole, you're welcome.' Honestly, he didn't know what to do. And the reason I say that is because I don't think he dared to do anything to any cop in this town, not after he had his conversation with Ralph Lamb. I mean, there were all sorts of things that floated around about the sheriff. But he was a stand-up guy when it came to taking care of that kind of business. He wasn't going to tolerate anybody running roughshod over his people."

Yet here came Sleeper, drawing a map on a chalkboard that zeroed in on a stately home in Paradise Palms that was squarely in the county sheriff's jurisdiction. Its owner, Las Vegas socialite Ava Pittman, was moving major amounts of heroin, he told the men in the room, and he was going to dress one of them as a florist and give him a delivery van so they could get close. Once the lead agent got into the house, he'd announce that a raid was under way, and the rest could follow.

"Anyone have a problem?" Sleeper asked the group he had assembled.

The agents looked at one another. No one said a word.

As the daylight city was cranking to life on February 21, 1970, the florist van pulled up to 1568 Pawnee Drive and the undercover walked to the intercom with a bouquet in his hands. He knew he was being watched on closed-circuit TV and calmly buzzed.

"Who's there?" a voice crackled through.

"Flowers for Ava," he replied.

"Come around to the side door," Ava Pittman said.

Pittman claimed to be a grandniece of Vail Pittman, the state's Democratic governor from 1945 to 1950, and she served various charitable causes; but her house was built like a fortress, with iron bars on the windows and the shades pulled down. The deliveryman made his way to the side and looked over both his shoulders. Then, when the service door opened just a crack, he threw his shoulder against it to push his way inside. As his colleagues stormed in after him, the fake florist threw down a search warrant and announced, "This is a raid."

Pittman stood helplessly with her mother as Sleeper's men tore through the place, tossing bedrooms, closets, and spare rooms. After an hour's worth of commotion, they ended up with sixty bags of 14.2 percent pure heroin—roughly three times street strength—a hundred methadone tablets, and a loaded M68 rifle that Pittman kept in her bedroom.

Lamb hit the roof when he heard about the raid. Who the hell was John Sleeper to show him up like that? While the *Sun* trumpeted the raid with the headline "Las Vegas Police Nab Narco Queen," Lamb screamed at the police chief and mayor to get that son of a bitch under control. Before the police chief,

Paul Wichter, could investigate, Sleeper poured fuel on the fire by holding an impromptu press conference in his office, where he stood over a table filled with the bindles of seized heroin. With reporters crowded around him, the buzz-cut cop accused Pittman of selling $33,000 worth of heroin to high school kids on a monthly basis. It took another week for Wichter to finally assert his power and demote Sleeper to a desk job in the detective's bureau.

"Vegas Police Chief Ousts Narco Buster," the *Sun* blared.

Sleeper's demotion concerned the black community leaders, who viewed him as a critical ally. On the Monday after the police chief announced his discipline, a group of black businessmen descended on City Hall, not to demand equal protection or any major new initiative, but to beg for the littlest bit of attention from the cops. "The possibility of inviting capital in is nil," a businessman named Bob Bailey complained. "We can't even get a black person to open a business here and black people are not going to black businesses. They are afraid to."

Bailey didn't specifically blame heroin for the "troublemakers who don't want to work at all." But he didn't have to. In most African American quarters, it was quietly believed that the city's Mormon elders were letting heroin finish what they'd started at the Moulin Rouge. Bailey ended his speech by saying, "We have one of the best law enforcement agencies in the country. But we just don't get any benefit from it over here."

Not surprisingly, Sleeper didn't take his punishment quietly. On the contrary, he ratcheted up his war with the sheriff's department, telling reporters that he felt duty-bound to roust Pittman because he'd learned she was giving protection money to Lamb's deputies. Even by Sleeper's eccentric standards, it was a remarkable statement. Not that it was implausible. Both police forces had corrupt elements. But Sleeper was going after the powerful sheriff where he knew it would hurt most: his law-and-order reputation.

"I can't imagine getting demoted for arresting suspected dope peddlers who we think are supplying kids in our schools," he announced. "But if that's what the politicians in this town want, they can have it."

What was only beginning to become clear was how far ahead the police lieutenant had planned. Even as some members of the city council were pushing for his ouster, he strode to a microphone on May 9 to announce that he was formally launching his bid to become the next sheriff of Clark County and replace Ralph Lamb. "I expect this campaign to be one of the most hard fought and controversial in Clark County," he said.

Painting himself as the last honest cop in Vegas, the demoted lieutenant confided that he'd been subpoenaed by DA George Franklin Jr. to tell a grand jury what he knew about payoffs. But, he said, he feared the invitation was really a thinly veiled way to "find out what I have on them so they could lock it up forever."

As performances went, it was bravura. The police lieutenant not only made himself out to be the last honest cop in Las Vegas—a role that Frank Serpico would soon play to even greater effect in New York—but also cast a net of suspicion over almost everyone in Las Vegas politics. Suddenly mothers with placards started materializing on the steps of City Hall, shouting, "We need Sleeper." Two deputies would be hauled into the grand jury and questioned at length about his claims.

Sonny had to be worried about these developments. Since he lived in the same neighborhood as Pittman, he would have followed the arrest closely, especially since the people of Paradise Palms weren't used to seeing SWAT teams swarming across their streets. It was the talk of the neighborhood.

And there was the startling involvement of the federal Bureau of Narcotics and Dangerous Drugs. The feds were supposed to be paying attention to things like casino skimming and mob hits, not a beautician who sold cocaine between romantic trysts or a charity doyen who specialized in selling heroin in high schools.

If the feds were going to start getting mixed up in cases like that, it represented a new and alarming escalation of the burgeoning drug war.

6.

THE BLEEDER

The port city of Bayonne, New Jersey, is a tough-talking ethnic enclave filled with Irish and Italians. The city is downtrodden in parts but full of family and community and always ready to defend its working-class sensibilities against its wealthier neighbor to the northeast.

In the summer of 1970, one of the most famous residents of Bayonne was a former Marine turned fighter, Chuck Wepner. The product of German, Ukrainian, and Polish stock, Wepner looked like an exaggerated version of the longshoremen who hung out on the Bay of Bayonne. "I used to be six-foot-one," he liked to quip, showing an easy way around a joke. "But with all those uppercuts, now I'm six-foot-five." Wepner, who sold wholesale liquor to pay his bills, wasn't the flashiest fighter in town, but he drew fans in his climb up the heavyweight ladder because of an unfortunately colorful tendency: he bled more than anyone else in the sport. The summer before, he lost a brutal decision against George Foreman at Madison Square Garden when he failed to get out of the way of a right cross. "My bone came right through my eye," he'd say in an interview. "That was a bad cut."

Wepner was co-managed by an ex-boxer, Gary Garafola, who ran a popular joint in nearby Union City called the Rag Doll. Long and narrow, with seventy-two stools around its bar and a pair of cages that featured go-go girls dancing in bikinis, the place was packed on weekends with a tough blue-collar crowd. Garafola was able to keep the peace because he could punch harder than most of his customers and it was generally known that he was a front for a powerful captain in the Genovese crime family, James Napoli.

Garafola was already under indictment in a case involving the theft of $80,000 worth of copper when his name came up in a bigger case involving Napoli, whom a New York grand jury accused of being the underworld king of fight fixing. According to prosecutors, Napoli met Garafola at a country club in the Catskills five days before his client, Frankie DePaula, was knocked down three times in the first round of a fight at Madison Square Garden. "How does everything look?" Napoli asked over dinner at the club. "Everything looks good," Garafola replied. "The kid will listen."

A second meeting occurred right after the loss at an Upper East Side restaurant in Manhattan. According to the indictment,

"Further testimony disclosed that, as Gary Garafola and the defendant [DePaula] were leaving the restaurant, Garafola asked the defendant if he had any small change for the hatcheck girl, and that the defendant replied, 'You're kidding, I scored today, man. All I got is hundreds.'"*

Since Bayonne's fight scene wasn't that large, it was inevitable that Garafola would recruit Wepner and that it would happen at the Rag Doll when he saw Wepner eyeing a go-go girl. "You like her?" he asked, handing Wepner the keys to his office. "I'll send her in." An hour later, when Wepner came out, Garafola was waiting to ask, "So, you want to sign with us or not?" As Wepner told me in his Bayonne apartment, "I took the pen and signed with him right there. And it was a very good move, because Gary was very influential."

Soon after Garafola signed Wepner, he asked his partner, a crotchety fight man named Al Braverman, to reach out to Ash Resnick, whom Braverman knew, to see if Sonny might be interested in facing their new client.

At that point Resnick was no longer managing fighters. But he sent the request to a friend who he thought might be interested: the Las Vegas boxing referee Davey Pearl. A few times a week Pearl would stop by Ottawa Drive to take Sonny on runs through the mountains or along the Sahara golf course. Like Geraldine, Pearl believed it was time for Sonny to retire. "Some-

---

*DePaula, who was Garafola's co-defendant in the theft case, was shot outside his girlfriend's apartment shortly after being acquitted. Garafola was indicted for the shooting but later acquitted.

day they're gonna write a blues song just for fighters," Sonny once said. "It'll be for slow guitar, soft trumpet, and a bell." But as soon as Pearl broached the interest from Braverman, he could see in Sonny's eyes that he wasn't ready to sing those blues.

While Pearl worked on getting Sonny a license to fight in New Jersey, there was no question about who would get him in fighting shape again. Las Vegas had only one true boxing gym, and on an afternoon in early May, Sonny drove his Caddy to the corner of West Charleston Boulevard and South Main Street and climbed the stairs to the Ringside Gym on the second floor to find Johnny Tocco.

When it came to the intersection of the mob and boxing, Tocco was the flashing light at the four-way stop. Everyone came through his gym—boxers, managers, mobsters and all their wannabes—because he kept it simple. He filled the room with heavy bags and the heavier aroma of smoke from the cigars he kept clenched in his teeth.

Tocco had a mile-wide soft spot for Sonny, who'd been coming to his gym since the fifties, but he also knew his friend took his physical gifts for granted. So before he agreed to train Liston for his fifty-fourth professional fight, Tocco put down a set of demands. The ex-champ had to run in the morning, then chop wood, go home for a nap, and come back to train in the afternoon. "Who says I ain't gonna do that?" Sonny told him, and the men had a deal.

Six weeks later Tocco, Sonny, and Pearl deplaned at Newark

Airport with Lem Banker, the Vegas gambler who ran the Sahara Health Club, and promptly headed to a hotel that had been reserved for them. The days of Resnick renting mansions were long gone. Their cab pulled up to a motel that was as much of a fleabag as North Bergen had to offer, with a thin coat of pale lime paint in the lobby and bumpy beds. Garafola arranged with the motel management for them to eat all they wanted for free, but as soon as Banker took one look at the restaurant, he said, "Come on, we're getting out of here," and took the group to a decent chophouse he knew a few towns over.

The group was literally mobbed the moment they walked in. Manhattan's sophisticates wouldn't be caught dead coming to New Jersey to see a fight. But, as Banker put it, "all the mob killers loved Sonny," and they gave him a hero's welcome as soon as he settled into a booth. Banker couldn't spend a dime of his own money on the thick steaks and red wine that were laid in front of them, and Sonny, whose sour mood had by then brightened, gladly shook hands with everyone who stopped by.

But there appeared to be more business than boxing going on during the stopover. "One of the guys came up to me afterwards and said Sonny asked him if he knew where he could move any hot money," Banker recalled. "I think he was in deep with some drug dealers on the Westside and was trying to do some deals on the side."

The anecdote raises an interesting question: Why would Sonny fly two thousand miles to fight in a dingy armory across the Hudson River if he didn't see another angle? It couldn't have been for the thirteen grand that Garafola and Braverman were offering, most of which he wound up giving Banker to repay a disastrous boxing bet he'd made in a desperate effort to manufacture some cash.

No, there had to be another reason, and it seems at least plausible that it had to do with the kind of deals that James Napoli was so adept at making. In an interview in the late 1990s, Tocco recalled sitting in the hotel's coffee shop with Sonny when a pair of toughs entered and motioned for Sonny to join them. The next day one of those men approached Tocco to tell him that he shouldn't feel bad if his boy lost the fight. "Chuck's a real popular guy here," the thug said.

In recalling the scene to the writer Nick Tosches for his book *The Devil and Sonny Liston*, Tocco said that he immediately confronted Sonny about what he'd promised the mob. "If something's going on, I want to know about it," he demanded.

"Aw, go to sleep," Sonny said. "I'm gonna knock this guy out."

When Wepner heard Sonny had agreed to fight him at the armory, he hugged his managers. His loss to Foreman had been a painful setback in more ways than one. He needed to put it out of people's minds.

To get ready, Wepner began his training at a place not far from the Rag Doll on Summit Avenue, Bufano's Gym and Pool Parlor. Its owner, Dominick Bufano, didn't have Tocco's big-fight pedigree, but he was smart and loyal and came up with a sensible plan. After watching Liston's fights over and over on a reel-to-reel, Bufano decided that while Sonny might not have had the finishing power he once had, Wepner couldn't afford his usual style of fighting from the inside. Instead, he'd have to weave in and out of Liston's remarkable eighty-two-inch reach using jabs and left-right combinations to wear him down. "I always trained real hard because I knew I didn't have a great deal of talent," Wepner says. "I had to get myself in great condition."

By prior agreement, Wepner got the gym from three in the afternoon until about six and then would vacate it for Sonny. But the first time Liston entered, Wepner made sure he was around so he could say hello. He did it with a simple "How you doin'?" Sonny, who'd been rude to plenty of more famous people, walked past him as if he didn't exist.

He kept up the silent treatment through the weigh-in, which was held at a picture-postcard establishment on Bergen Avenue in Jersey City called the Oyster Bay Restaurant. The first time Wepner had laid eyes on Sonny, he was struck by how much older he looked than on the old fight films. His birth certificate may have said thirty-eight but Sonny's face had the creased look of a man of fifty. Now, however, as Sonny took off his robe, Wepner understood why he fascinated other fighters. His body looked at least a dozen years younger. All of a sudden Wepner began reevaluating whether he'd done enough training after all.

After the weigh-in, the men were led to a stage for the obligatory press conference. Wepner was in his glory, but Sonny managed to insult both his hosts in New Jersey and their rivals across the river in New York when he was asked if he hoped the ban against him in the Big Apple would be lifted so he could fight there as well. "New York can go to hell," he replied. "I don't need New York because I'm on my way down, anyway."

On June 29, it seemed all of Jersey City was collected outside the armory, a cavernous red stone WPA-era structure built in 1937 that took up an entire city block. Since the state hadn't had a major fight in seven years—when Joey Giardello beat Dick Tiger in Atlantic City—Abe Greene, the athletic commissioner, walked the grounds telling anyone who'd listen that this was the beginning of a new era for New Jersey. Wepner certainly hoped it would be a new era for him. Before the crowds started settling in, he approached Barney Felix, the referee who'd also handled ring duties at the first Liston–Ali bout, and said, "Do me a favor, Barney. I'm a rough fighter, I get cut once in a while. Just make sure you talk to the doctor first before you do anything." He said this because he knew his reputation for bleeding preceded him and because the official fight doctor, Reginald Farrar, was a friend of his. As Wepner told me, "I knew that Reggie wasn't going to stop the fight on a small cut. I was going to have to really be cut open."

As the fight time neared, Wepner was in his dressing room, answering reporters' questions, when a roar went up outside. "It's Muhammad Ali," someone said, and the pack of reporters raced out. Surely enough, Ali had come by unannounced.

Ali ducked the questions that came at him, insisting he'd just driven down from Philadelphia to see a fight, and happily signed autographs for anyone who called him by his Muslim name. (He ignored those who kept calling him Clay.) "That fucker just won't go away," Liston complained to Banker, summarizing a decade's worth of grievances.

There was only one camera in the armory and it was perched so high above the ring that those who later saw the footage would have to settle for seeing two fuzzy figures circling in muted black-and-white. Wepner, who weighed in at 228, had a four-inch height advantage. But Liston's body, lacquered and shiny, continued to inspire Wepner to envy. His shoulders folded over on themselves and his stomach looked smooth, as if it had never been touched.

At the opening bell, Wepner tried to put all that out of his mind and sailed into that stomach with a walloping left hook that he followed by a flurry of combinations. His goal was to move Sonny into a corner of the ring, but Sonny wasn't so easily moved: he staked out the center using his enormous reach to whack at Wepner's head with the jab. Wepner had the curiously detached sense of hearing the pain without feeling it. Every time Liston connected, an explosion went off in his ear canal but he wasn't registering any actual agony. Instead he kept coming at Sonny, his leaden feet surprisingly nimble, driven by adrenaline.

Felix gave Sonny the first two rounds, but Wepner fought to a draw in the third and then rallied to win the next two. "Press him!" Braverman shouted hoarsely as the sixth round wore on. But Wepner's face was beginning to bloat, and Sonny had no intention of drawing things out with body shots. Using Wepner's aggressiveness against him, he waited until Wepner tried to jab and then circled in under his punch, flattening Wepner's chin with an uppercut and going to work on his head. The closing seconds of the sixth featured a pair of impacts that rocked Wepner's head clear back to his shoulders; by the time it bobbed back, Sonny butted his head up into it, opening a pair of gashes over Wepner's eyes.

"My right eye, I can't see out of it!" Wepner screamed when he came back to his stool.

"You got a left eye—use it," Braverman shot back.

"And my nose. I can't breathe out of my nose. I think it's broken."

"You got a mouth, don't you?" Braverman replied, continuing his wellspring of useful advice.

By the eighth round, Wepner was fighting shadows. When he threw a left hook that was so far off the mark that it glanced Felix's shoulder, the referee stopped the action. "Come on, Barney," Wepner pleaded. "Gimme another round here."

"Your eyes are all busted up, you can't see," Felix said.

Wepner kept pleading, so Felix raised three fingers and asked Wepner to tell him how many he had up. Braverman, sitting behind his fighter, tapped him three times. "Three!" Wepner shouted excitedly.

By the ninth round Wepner's face was a mask of matted blood and his eye sockets were pools of darkness. Sure, it would have made Sonny's life easier if Felix stopped the fight in the eighth. But as long as the fight was going on, his job was to stare into the mess and make it messier. At the end of the ninth, it looked like the entire top could be lifted off Wepner's head. What was it that Wepner said about the fight doctor? "I knew that Reggie wasn't going to stop the fight on a small cut. I was going to have to really be cut open."

He was that cut open.

After the doctor ended the bout and Sonny changed out of his striped shorts into a natty charcoal-gray suit, he stopped by Wepner's dressing room to say "Good fight." They weren't warm words, but they were a kind of admiration for the punishment he'd put himself through.

"Hey, Sonny," a reporter said. "Is he the bravest guy you ever fought?"

"No," Sonny deadpanned. "His manager is."

Wepner, who was running a 107-degree fever and suffering from what would later be diagnosed as clinical shock, was incredulous that the fight had been stopped. "They let me bleed for five rounds. Why couldn't they give me a chance to win by a knockout in the last round?" he asked.

His wife, Phyllis, answered by driving him to the emergency room, where he received seventy-two stitches. It took another two days for the fever to finally break and a couple more weeks for Wepner to feel human again.

Before Sonny boarded his TWA flight back home, a reporter had asked him what was in store next. "I'd quit boxing if I had another source of income," he said with weary candor. Now, settling into his seat, he reached into the bag of cash that he'd been given at the armory and pulled out ten thousand dollars to repay the ill-fated bet he'd made to Banker. Then he rummaged around for the rest and handed three thousand more to Tocco.

Whatever other deals he'd struck in Jersey City would have to be paid off when he was back home.

It's worth pausing halfway through 1970, with most of the major events yet to come, to see Sonny as he put the key in the lock of his Ottawa Drive home and threw down his bags after his trip home from Jersey City.

Six months earlier, his career was moribund. Now, if he wasn't reborn, he at least felt redeemed. Don Chargin at the Grand Olympic Auditorium in Los Angeles was calling to offer $35,000 or a percentage of the gate—whichever was higher—for him to face a newcomer, José Luis García. (The Venezuelan had just floored the previously undefeated Ken Norton.) And there was another, even more glamorous offer from the UK fighter Joe Bugner, who wanted him to come to Europe, something he hadn't done since his second victory against Floyd Patterson and dearly wanted to do again.

Yep, things were looking up. So he threw down his bags, gassed up the Caddy in the garage, and took a nine-minute drive to heaven.

With the July Fourth weekend approaching, the casinos in Vegas were busy changing their marquees. Totie Fields was now at the Riviera, Jack Jones was settling into the Sands with Jo Anne Worley of *Laugh-In* fame, and Don Rickles was at the Parkway Theater. Poor Jimmy Durante keeled over while performing at the Frontier Hotel. But Vic Damone agreed to pitch in for him, so everyone seemed to be happy. Also, Perry

Como was saying good-bye after a successful run at the International to make room for Glen Campbell and the Goodtime Hour Singers.

There was also a grab bag of come-ons for the tourists expected to descend for the holiday weekend. At the Aladdin, you could drink all you wanted for $2.25 a person, while Caesars was advertising its happy hour with an illustration of a cocktail waitress holding a martini glass and lying on her stomach, her bikini uniform pushed halfway down her derriere, with the caption "Bottoms up '70."

When Sonny got another new Cadillac in the beginning of 1970, his sparring partner Gary Bates saw how much he loved it and suggested he get personalized plates. "Why?" Sonny shot back. "So Geraldine can follow me wherever I go?" It was with that mind-set that he drove down East Flamingo and up Spencer Street, to the development where Bates lived, Central Park West. Bates had a unit in the back but Sonny wasn't there to see his pal. He was there to see a woman who lived across the lot, in a bungalow shaded by trees.

James Baldwin once wrote of Sonny that while "there is a great deal of violence in him, I sensed no cruelty at all. On the contrary, he reminded me of big, black men I have known who acquired the reputation of being tough in order to conceal the fact that they weren't hard. Anyone who cared to could turn them into taffy."

Barbara C. was the woman who turned Sonny into taffy. As Bates would recall, "She had all the equipment for a showgirl. Big eyes. Big boobs. Big hips. The whole deal." Lem Banker, offering his own description, added: "He fell in love with some girl. Brunette. Buxom. Not a skinny girl. He met her at the Flamingo. She looked like Jennifer Jones. She was at least fifteen years younger than Sonny. She knew she was fucking a married man."*

Bates knew when Sonny was visiting because he could see his Caddy parked outside her window. Sometimes Sonny would knock on his door if she wasn't home and hang out until she arrived. Bates told me this story:

"I had a girlfriend who was pissed because she came to town months after we'd broken up and I was dating other people. She knocked on the door and when I opened it she called me a no-good, rotten, cheating son of a bitch. Then she took a rat-tailed comb out of her purse—you know, the kind with a handle— and *whack*, hit me right under the eyebrow. Sonny was standing outside talking to Barbara and this chick ran past him and threw the comb at his feet. Sonny told Barbara to get a towel and some ice. Then he asked me, 'Did you know her?' I said, 'Yeah, I dated her for a while.' He looked me square in the eye and said, 'I'd quit that bitch.' That was what he said: 'I'd quit that bitch.'"

On one hand, there was nothing terribly surprising about Sonny's choice for a mistress. He preferred white women to black

---

*I made multiple attempts to find Barbara C. The Culinary Workers Union, which covers cocktail waitresses, had only one listing in its 1969 and 1970 archives that matched her name. But when I reached the woman, she said she'd never met Sonny and didn't know another cocktail waitress who shared her name. Police records, database searches, and old phone records were also unavailing. If she's still alive, she is as elusive today as she seemed to be then.

women. Bates recalls picking up his friend for a night of carousing and finding that Sonny was genuinely irritated when he suggested they go to a black strip club. "What makes you think I want black pussy?" he said.

What was more revealing about their affair was what it said about the hidden world of Las Vegas. In the early hours of the morning, a racially divided city turned color-blind in the cheap motels and housing developments where an aging fighter could find true love under a casino queen's tinsel dress. It was a dim payoff for a lifetime of beatings. But it was the reason plenty of people came to Vegas. And Sonny was no exception.

Part II

LOVE,
AMERICAN
STYLE

(previous page)

Sonny Liston on the set of *Moonfire* in 1970.

(Courtesy Michael Parkhurst)

7.

FABULOUS
LAS VEGAS

FROM "Criswell Predicts,"
Fabulous Las Vegas, July 25, 1970

I predict that a gaping hole created by a meteor hitting the South Pacific will be a major marvel of the New Year! . . . I predict that the old radio show Amos and Andy will return as a TV series next season! . . . I predict that a new way of highway construction will save the taxpayers millions of dollars. . . . I predict that Art Linkletter's "People Are Funnier Than Ever!" based on his TV interviews will hit the best seller lists. . . . I predict that Canada will soon deport all American boys who sought refuge from the draft but entered the drug market and petty theft. . . . I predict that a new medicine out of Germany will dissolve the fatty tissues in your body in a safe and sane manner! . . . I predict the cast of a very famous daytime soap opera will soon experience a plague that turns their hair purple! I predict many startling innovations for your TV viewing.

In the summer of 1970, no pair of personalities loomed over Las Vegas more than the billionaire archrivals who were battling to buy every square inch of it: Kirk Kerkorian and Howard Hughes.

Kerkorian wasn't widely known when he made his first big deal in 1962, plowing $960,000 into eighty vacant acres just off Highway 91 in what would eventually be regarded as the greatest land grab in Las Vegas history. But he was wildly ambitious. The son of Armenian parents who had lost all of their land during the Great Depression, he was scarred by a childhood in which they found themselves moving every three months because they could not afford rent. Kerkor—his original first name—made spare change as an amateur boxer in his teens. But it wasn't until he became obsessed with flying, and took a job paying a thousand dollars a month to ferry pilots for the Royal Canadian Air Force, that he had the means to finance his ambitions. He first bought his own plane and then built a small charter service into a national carrier that he sold in 1968 for an $85 million profit. Using the cash from that sale, he bought a stake in MGM Studios, a Hollywood institution that still had high name recognition and great stars under contract. Then he went to war with Howard Hughes.

Hughes was already on a spending spree in Las Vegas. In four years he'd gobbled up the Desert Inn along with the Cast-aways and the Frontier, which were across the street, and the Silver Slipper and Dunes. In all, he had a quarter of the beds on the Strip. But Kerkorian had an ingenious idea.

With the land that he bought a half mile east of the Strip, on Paradise Road, he decided to build a lavish resort that tourists could reach on a straight line from McCarran Airport without ever passing all that prime real estate that Hughes assembled on the Strip. As Hughes biographers Donald L. Barlett and James B. Steele wrote, "Kerkorian's publicity angered Hughes. It threatened to overshadow his own bid to become Nevada's premier gambler, it bruised his fragile ego, and it meant more competition for the tourist dollar."

But by the time Hughes realized what Kerkorian was up to, it was too late to stop him. Hughes made several ill-fated attempts to convince Kerkorian to scale back his plans, at one point insisting that the underground atomic tests under way in the desert would cause untold damage to a hotel as massive as the International. But it was to no avail. In desperation, Hughes gobbled up the Landmark, an infamous eyesore across the street from the International's building site. The vacant building had a glass elevator that ran up its narrow spire to a spaceshiplike top that offered a panoramic view of the city, and Hughes reopened it a day before the International was scheduled to open its doors on July 2,

1969, with a gala featuring four hundred celebrity guests. But much to Hughes's consternation, the International still got all the buzz. Limousines choked Paradise Road for its unveiling and confetti rained down on an inaugural that featured Barbra Streisand. Beaten to the PR punch, Hughes had no choice but to sit back in his darkened room at the Desert Inn and hope with all the malice he could muster that Kerkorian had overplayed his hand.

Since no one had seen Hughes in years, it was easy to call Kerkorian the more glamorous figure. But he really was. He wore his bushy brown hair slicked up and favored turtlenecks and wool jackets. His smile ran the length of his face and his eyes were pools of brown. His salesmanship and self-made story turned him into a golden boy on Wall Street, which had helped him leverage his MGM acquisition. But Kerkorian was burning through cash. Not only had he put $16 million of his own money into his hotel, he was in hock to European investors who were charging him a fortune in daily interest.

Desperate for a new round of financing, Kerkorian went to the U.S. Securities and Exchange Commission for a bailout. The agency had helped him in February 1969 when it green-lighted his request to sell 17 percent of his company at $5 a share, netting him a $60 million haul. But now, a year later, its lawyer balked at his request.

The reason may have had to do with two investigations that were suddenly raising questions about Kerkorian's ties to organized crime.

In the first case, the SEC was taking a fresh look at his 1967 purchase of the Flamingo Hotel. He'd bought the Flamingo to raid its staff for the International. But the government's attorneys wanted to know whether he had also purposely hid the secret ownership stake that Meyer Lansky kept after Bugsy Siegel was shot dead. Just as damaging were a pair of tapes from 1962 that suddenly fell into the hands of a New York legislative committee. In the first, Kerkorian could be heard offering to travel from California to New York to deliver $20,300 to Charlie "The Blade" Tourine, the same gangster who the FBI believed had his hooks in Ash Resnick. (According to Resnick's FBI dossier, he introduced Kerkorian to Tourine in Miami, and helped Tourine take many of Kerkorian's biggest bets.) In the second tape, Tourine was overheard calling Kerkorian "a real nice guy."

The fallout was devastating. Kerkorian released a statement through his attorney denying that he had ever "knowingly been associated with any member of a criminal organization." But when the SEC decided to delay his second public offering, the price of his International Leisure company stock went into a free fall.

Did Hughes have anything to do with the twin investigations? He certainly had enough influence in the Nixon administration to reach into the SEC. And unearthing a long-lost tape was just his style. But whether he engineered the setback or simply had a healthy case of schadenfreude, the result was the same. He watched Kerkorian scramble to unload his beloved International.

The nation's brand-name hoteliers didn't stay away from the Strip strictly because they were concerned about their pristine images. They stayed away because of a law that required each stockholder in a company to undergo a thorough background check by the Nevada Gaming Control Board. The law was meant to deter investments by organized crime, but it also deterred the major hotel chains from investing in Las Vegas, because it wasn't practical for them to subject their stockholders to the Nevada rule. With Kerkorian on the ropes, Governor Paul Laxalt removed that requirement.

Suddenly free to negotiate, the biggest names in the business swept in with bailout offers for Kerkorian. Hyatt was the first, but Hilton was the most aggressive, and in mid-July, Barron Hilton announced that he had bought 37.5 percent of the International with a second round of 12.5 percent to follow, for $45 million in cash.

Kerkorian's lawyer tried to play down the sale by saying it was simply a way for his client to "get a partner on the reservations side of the business." Still, it was hard not to see the sale as a clear victory for Hughes, who'd dispensed with an archrival.*

It was also another sign of a tonal shift in the city. The Vietnam War was tearing America apart. But with Hughes and now the Hiltons in charge, Las Vegas was slipping back in time. One only had to read the reviews in the *Sun* by its entertainment columnist, Ralph Pearl, to realize how nostalgic the city was becoming. Raving about a show by the fifty-eight-year-old comedian Danny Thomas, Pearl wrote, "The young breed of so called café performer entering the saloon circuit these days could

---

* Kerkorian's setback was only temporary. He came back in 1973 with his finances stronger and built the MGM Grand, to once again have the largest hotel on the Strip. While his personal fortune at one point climbed as high as $18 billion, *Forbes* estimated that when he died at the age of ninety-eight in June 2015, it had dwindled to $4 billion.

learn many lessons watching this masterful hook nose mesmerize the losers, boozers and lovers as he played the actor, the clown, the friendly neighbor next door."

There was also little tolerance for edgy, countercultural humor, as the comedian George Carlin found out. The Frontier had always been the kind of place where you could take the wife for a steak and scotch. But on a Wednesday night in September, the crowd was horrified to hear a profanity-laced tirade from the comedian, who was promptly fired for his routine about the seven dirty words you couldn't say on TV.

All of this might have played into Sonny's hands if he'd been willing to be the lovable, nostalgic figure that hoteliers like the Hiltons wanted—more like his friend, Joe Louis. But just the opposite was true. Without a new fight on the horizon, or a reason to rein himself in, Sonny was freely indulging his appetites and grievances while overestimating how safe he would be in this safe haven of retro values.

To turn on the television in the summer of 1970 was to hear everyone shouting over everyone else. The ground troops that Richard Nixon sent into Cambodia were shouting over exploding shrapnel. Congress was shouting at the president. And the president was shouting at the nation's college students to end their protests over a bloody seven-day period in which thousands of U.S. ground troops were sent into Cambodia and a hundred bombers were unleashed over the skies of North Vietnam. In a somber twenty-two-minute address to the nation that spring, the president swore that he needed to draft another 150,000 soldiers to accommodate the invasion of Cambodia.

In the halls of Congress, members of Nixon's own party were horrified at the way he'd doubled the size of the conflict overnight. "Unbelievable" was how Oregon senator Mark Hatfield put it. "Ghastly," added his Republican colleague from New York, Charles Goodell.

With widespread protests breaking out across the country, Nixon decided to double down on the domestic crime-fighting initiative that his advisors were pushing. In a playbook called "Prognosis for the 1972 Election," they argued that to win a second term while conducting an unpopular war, Nixon would need to single-handedly prosecute "the most massive effort to control crime in the nation's history."

His advisors had already coalesced around the idea of a domestic drug war as the centerpiece of that policy. The question was how to wage it. Drugs were traditionally the province of local police, but Nixon needed something federal, something that he could control. And he found exactly what he was looking for in a tiny agency that for most of its existence had been lampooned as bumbling and ineffective.

The Bureau of Narcotics was formed in the early 1900s to regulate doctors who used opium to treat addicts. Even though it was made famous by the 1947 movie *T-Men*, it veered between scandal—officers were arrested from time to time for taking bribes—and irrelevance. As recently as 1968, it had just 330 agents working around the country in mostly administrative jobs, which put it on the far fringes of the action.

Congress tried to help the agency by merging it with the Bureau of Drug Abuse Control, a tiny offshoot of the Department of Health, Education, and Welfare that monitored doctors and pharmacists who overprescribed pills. But the newly named Bureau of Narcotics and Dangerous Drugs (BNDD) had no deep networks of sources, experienced undercover agents, or the wherewithal to mount extended operations.

Ironically, that was what made it perfect for Nixon. He could reinvent the office from the ground up and, most important, make it answer to him. It would be his tool and his legacy, and he signed a memo that ensured it would have all the clout it needed. Any other agency that had a hand in drug enforcement would have to back off. The BNDD would have the singular responsibility of investigating narco-trafficking around the world. To fulfill his mandate, Nixon gave the agency a 50 percent budget increase and sent it out to hire some real shit kickers.

All of which was how John Sutton came to work for the federal government.

At the age of thirty, Sutton was already a legend on the streets of Compton, California. A towering man with a fifty-seven-inch chest, the former Marine came to the police force after earning a criminal justice degree from Cal State, and from the moment he was hired he tried to be the sharpest-dressed, best-armed, meanest cop on the force.

Because his muscular frame pinched against the fabric of his uniform, Sutton desperately tried to get out of it and into street clothes from the moment he arrived. He lobbied his precinct captain for more dangerous work until he eventually was rewarded with an assignment to join a task force that was looking into a gun-running ring. Thrilled to finally be doing what he considered important work, he bought a tan leather jacket with wide lapels and a brimmed hat that he moved around until he found the perfect way to tilt it to one side. On the night of his first big undercover assignment, Sutton drove a Ford LTD with a trunk full of hundred-dollar bills to a vacant lot on the far side of town to meet two suspects. He expected his heart to be beating out of his chest, but he found himself strangely calm as the hoods opened their car's trunk to reveal a cache of machine guns. With backup sharpshooters hidden on rooftops, Sutton bought a dozen of the automatic weapons for $10,000. In that moment the idea that he could be shot to death if something went wrong didn't occur to him at all.

His performance that day led to a second assignment, involving a local methamphetamine lab with ties to the Mexican cartels. This time, instead of a midnight meet alone, the plan was for him to join a group of agents to go into the lab with their guns hot. "I was used to seeing the way they did it on TV," Sutton told me. "On TV the cops were always running into someplace with their guns drawn, yelling, 'Freeze, motherfucker, federal agent! If you move we'll blow your goddamn head off!'" But, as he learned that night, any agent who had to talk that much was already halfway to dead. The feds he was with launched the raid by throwing a blinding stun grenade into the lab, nearly ripping its roof off as they broke down the door. By the time the drug dealers squeezed the blinding light out of their eyes, they were already in cuffs.

In late 1969, with the BNDD ramping up its hiring, Sutton sent a résumé to the agency and within a few weeks found himself being interviewed in its Los Angeles field office. The job paid only $10,000, but that was still more than the median income, and as long as gas stayed at thirty-five cents and you could buy a new home for $29,000, it was plenty. On the basis of his work in Compton, Sutton was hired that fall to join the bureau, which already included Bill Alden, the special agent who'd helped pull off the arrest of Earl Cage in Vegas and was present when Sonny got set free.

Once he entered the bureau's training academy, a whole new world opened up for Sutton. The thirty-year-old trained in hand-to-hand combat, shooting high-powered firearms, and discreetly following cars at a distance. But what really excited him were the latest technological gizmos that the feds were using. There were parabolic microphones that picked up suspects' conversations from miles away, and infrared video. There was also his favorite, a covert automated tracking system, a shoe box–size device that fit in a vehicle's car and allowed the feds to track it by radar.

When he finally arrived in the BNDD's Los Angeles office on Olympic Boulevard and Figueroa Street, Sutton could feel the energy. The floor was divided into rows of cubicles that hummed with the sound of computers paid for by the new budget increases and a hundred agents with badges dangling from their belts. Some were coming off undercover shifts in bell-bottoms and paisley shirts, while others were dressed like bikers and yet others seemed most comfortable in their government-issue gray. They all had the esprit de corps of a group that was about to start something big and for a high purpose that went all the way up to the White House. Drinking in the energy, Sutton felt at home for the first time in his police career.

In July of 1970, after just a few months on the job, Sutton already had a dozen cases and was eager to pick up more. He was particularly eager when his supervisor dropped a file on his desk that was referred from the BNDD's satellite office in Las Vegas. The file was about Sonny Liston.

After Alden's brush with the boxer more than a year earlier, the BNDD's office quietly opened its own investigation and, according to the intelligence packet, learned he was moving cocaine and quite possibly heroin out of the keno room in the International. The file was labeled "Significant Target of Opportunity." Looking at his calendar, Sutton decided to schedule a trip toward the end of the summer, when the desert wasn't so hot. In the meantime he'd study up on his subject.

After the Wepner fight, Sonny got a call from a friend in Arizona. "I need you back," Mike Parkhurst said. "We need to finish our movie."

Among the strange people that Sonny Liston collected, Mike Parkhurst was one of the strangest. He wasn't even thirty and already he'd made a small fortune publishing *Overdrive*, a magazine that featured scantily clad women posing on top of big rigs.

Parkhurst fancied himself the Hugh Hefner of the trucking set. He worked in an old Hollywood estate that had been over-run by hippie squatters and turned it into a luxury bed-and-breakfast for long haulers. In a spasm of optimism, he added a swimming pool, Tahitian bar, theater, game room, library, and formal dining room. He even hired a chef who'd once worked for Elizabeth Taylor. But to really build an empire, the budding mogul decided that he needed a film division, too. So he sat down to write a movie about Nazis and truckers and went to New York to sell it.

The financiers who met Parkhurst at Paramount Studios had trouble sharing his certainty that big-riggers would turn out for a low-budget movie about Nazis, and politely thanked him for his time. That might have been the end of it except that, as he was walking the city to clear his head, Parkhurst found himself on Forty-second Street in Times Square, looking up at some-thing that he instantly realized was the answer to his problem. It was a marquee for a new movie, *Head*, that featured the Mon-kees. In big black letters, it read: "Featuring: Sonny Liston."*

The Idea struck him like a bolt.

Sonny Liston! Of course! He's just who I need to cast in my movie about truckers and Nazis!

"It took me a while to track him down," Parkhurst told me years later. "But I finally got him on the line and he agreed to

---

* That movie was an odd bit of business. The actor Jack Nicholson sat down with his friend Bob Rafelson, the creator of the Monkees, and came up with a senseless series of set pieces. Writing in *The New York Times*, Vincent Canby advised: "'Head' . . . might be a film to see if you have been smoking grass or if you like to scream at the Monkees, or if you are inter-ested in what interests drifting heads and hysteric high school girls."

meet me at a hotel in Century City for breakfast." The young mogul patiently explained his idea for the movie over eggs and coffee, and while Sonny didn't exactly understand all the exigencies of the plot, he smiled. After all, not only was Parkhurst willing to give him six thousand dollars just for signing on to the project, he opened up his roadhouse to let Sonny train. What could be better?

The mansion gave Sonny a place to crash in Los Angeles away from Geraldine. If he wanted a hooker, Parkhurst got him a hooker. If he wanted a meal late at night, Liz Taylor's cook was happy to whip it up. There was sex and drugs and rock and roll around and then there was Sonny, somehow seamlessly blending right into the mix.

In the summer of 1969, when Parkhurst finally pulled together enough money to start shooting in the Arizona desert, the whole thing seemed like a vacation. One night Sonny got into a fight over a woman that turned into a bar brawl when a regular broke a beer bottle over his head and opened such a gash that Parkhurst was sure it would delay filming. To his amazement, it was barely noticeable a couple of days later. "I'd never seen anyone heal that fast," he'd say.

Another night, the actor Chuck Napier went out with Sonny, looking for a whorehouse. They were having trouble finding one until Sonny ordered Napier to pull up beside a gang of toughs, grabbed the biggest one, and announced, "I'm lookin' for pussy and you gonna show me where to find it." The next morning Napier pointed to Sonny in front of Parkhurst and said, "Going out with that guy's an adventure."

That first stretch of filming lasted until Parkhurst ran out of money, at which point he dispersed the cast, vowing to get more. By the summer of 1970 he had enough to get the job done.

After the Wepner fight, Sonny welcomed any kind of a paycheck, and the new scenes didn't require a lot of memorization. Parkhurst cast his daughter as a little girl who was eating an ice cream cone at a road stop when a bunch of rowdy bikers pulled up and frightened her. In perhaps one of the worst action scenes ever filmed, Sonny grabbed her with one hand and pulled a rider to the ground as the others roared past, cursing at him. Parkhurst thought the scene was over when his daughter recited the line "Do you want any ice cream?" But Sonny broke up the set by erupting in laughter.

It was said over and over again that Sonny loved children. Oftentimes it was said to mask an insult, as when someone suggested that he had a child's mind. But that robbed him of the one part of himself that he held dear: the part that sent him to orphanages and hospital wards when no one was looking, or that inspired him to show up to a kid's home with a swing set and a smile. Part of that may have been prompted by guilt over the way he treated Geraldine's two daughters when they first got married. Sonny at least initially tried to be chivalrous and claim Arletha and Eleanor for his own. But he was never the father they needed, and by the time the girls were in their teens they concluded that it was better to live outside their stepfather's shadow than be smothered by it.

As a result of all that, Geraldine accepted Daniel, whose mother may have spent as little as a night with Sonny, into her home; she desperately wanted to try to start a family one last time. In his own way, Sonny wanted to try, too, and on the day that she visited the set with Daniel he decided to do something special. When one of the actors suggested that he take his family to see a bullfight, Sonny brightened. He'd never been to one before. The actor, Roger Galloway, knew the manager of a ring in Nogales, Mexico, and offered to drive them. They all piled into his car for the ninety-minute drive across the border.

Once they arrived, Galloway introduced Sonny to the manager, who was astonished to be standing in the presence of the world-famous former heavyweight champion of the world. "Anything for you, my friend, anything," he said as he led the visitors to his president's box.

Before the group could settle in, the manager was announcing them to a standing ovation and the first matador was kneeling before Sonny in full regalia, extending his cape in a sign of deep veneration. When the bullfight began, Sonny kept Daniel on his lap, pointing out what was happening so the boy would understand why the bull was being stabbed. Afterward, the matador approached his box again, this time with the ear of the bull, and Sonny found himself choking up. He was at his most natural in public when he was angry, or at the very least resentful. Senator Estes Kefauver. J. Edgar Hoover. Ali. They'd all used Sonny to make a point, to justify their worldviews. And Sonny made it easy by not having a worldview to throw back at them. Jack Johnson was defined by his era's Jim Crow mentality. Joe Louis was propelled by World War II. Muhammad Ali turned his moment into a movement. All that Sonny had was his reputation as a thug who stumbled into a championship and didn't know what to do with it once he got it.

He couldn't defend himself with speeches because he hated public speaking. And he couldn't charm his way through the tough spots because he couldn't be charming, at least in front of large groups. (Get him alone with a cocktail waitress and you saw a different Sonny.) The easiest and most natural reaction was for him to become surly and suspicious. You could debate nature and nurture. But it was what it was.

Except now it wasn't. Here, in the most unlikely of places—a Mexican bullring, with his wife beside him and his son sitting on his lap—there were no critics. Just men with a deep respect for what he'd accomplished. They all knew that sometimes you get the bull and sometimes the bull gets you. And for an afternoon they could let Sonny forget about politics, about Muhammad Ali, and about the feds who wouldn't let Sonny forget his earlier mistakes.

After the bullfight was over, he lingered for an hour, doing something he never did: signing autographs and shaking hands. He was thrilled that Daniel could see him like this, and Geraldine stood back proudly. Finally, when he was done, he climbed back into Galloway's car for the ride back to Tucson. Stretching his long arms around Geraldine, he looked out at the passing view and said, "This was a good day."

8.

———

JONESING

As he packed his trumpet for an out-of-town gig, Robert Chudnick was blunt with his son: "I don't want you hanging around Sonny anymore."

The arrest of Ava Pittman, so close to them in Paradise Palms, had unnerved the musician in a way that his son, Mark, wasn't used to seeing. The old man was laying off big burglaries, cutting off deadbeat customers, and refusing to take new ones. He even gave his crew a little extra to make sure they remained loyal. The sheriff's race, with its emphasis on heroin and property crime, was leading both candidates to deploy all their resources in a contest to see who could get the biggest preelection headlines. With so much manpower on the street, all it would take was one mistake to bring them down. And, increasingly, Chudnick had come to believe that Sonny was the one who was going to make that mistake.

When Chudnick visited Sonny and saw a car parked nearby that he thought could be a cop doing surveillance, he stopped knocking on the door. Instead he let himself be seen visiting an acquaintance down the street and then secretly circled back to 2058 Ottawa Drive through the golf course. But even that had become too risky. A member of his crew had recently dealt to someone who OD'd and the sheriff's department narcotics unit was nosing around.

"I don't need Sonny's problems, okay?" he said, putting his trumpet into its velvet-lined case. "If he calls while I'm away, just hang up. Tell him I'll be in touch. Tell him anything. I just don't want him coming over here. There's no telling if we're being watched or he's being watched. Maybe we're all being watched. Just keep him fucking away, okay?"

Mark nodded obediently. The last time he'd seen Sonny was when they'd ended up in that bar on the North Side and Mark waited in the car for an hour, making him late getting home with the day's collection. His dad was still furious about that. It was a miracle Mark didn't get robbed.

"I'll be back in a week, two tops," he said. "Just lay low and things will be fine." The teen followed his father's advice, and for a few days things did stay quiet. But once Sonny heard that Red was out of town, he showed up on the Rodneys' doorstep.

"It had been a while. I was kind of glad to see him," Mark would tell me. But then he realized that Sonny was sweating and shaking and he wasn't looking at the man he knew. He was looking at something at once stranger and more familiar: a junkie who was jonesing.

"Where's your dad?" Sonny snarled. "Is he hiding from me?"

"No, no, man, he's out of town," Mark said, taking a very small step back.

He could see that Sonny's pupils were tiny, as if there was just one thing they could focus on, and he tried to distract his former sidekick with small talk. "So how's the fighting, man? Got anything lined up?" But Sonny wasn't interested in being distracted. He filled the doorway with his enormous frame and growled, "You got something for me?"

Mark kept a small stash for his personal use in a dresser in his room, apart from the larger quantities that his dad had buried in the backyard, and he fetched it for Sonny, who by then had moved into the living room. Sonny grabbed it and put his forefinger inside the baggie, letting a taste touch his lips. It was real, all right. But there was so little that he shoved it in his pocket and started tearing through the house, looking for more. He looked in Chudnick's bedroom, the basement, the kitchen. Still not convinced that Mark was telling the truth, he returned to the living room and backed the teen up against the wall. "Where's your dad?" he said again, this time expecting a different answer.

It was a threshold moment, the kind you either came back from or didn't. The two were alone. Plenty of bad stuff could happen at that hour of the night. But all at once something seemed to snap in Sonny's mind, as if he'd adjusted a mental kink. Maybe it was the fear on Mark's face. "I'll tell you what, I was plenty scared," he told me. Or maybe, just maybe, Sonny wasn't so far gone that he was willing to threaten a kid.

Whatever the reason, Sonny collected himself, muttered thanks for the heroin, and left without saying another word.

If there was one person who might have been able to save Sonny from himself, it was his friend and neighbor Joe Louis.

After Sonny knocked out Patterson in 1962, he called Louis "the greatest champion of all and my idol. He did everything I want to do. I intend to follow the example he set."

That turned out to be harder than Sonny imagined, mainly because Joe just seemed to be naturally better at everything. To start, Joe was outwardly friendlier. When a tourist approached him in the lobby of Caesars Palace to ask for an autograph, thinking he was the retired Brooklyn Dodgers star Don Newcombe, Joe quietly asked a friend how to spell the pitcher's name. Then he signed it without ever correcting the fan.

By contrast, when a middle-aged woman approached Sonny while he was playing blackjack at the Frontier and said, "You're Sonny Liston!" he replied, "Yeah, I knew that." The *Esquire* writer Bruce Jay Friedman captured Louis and Liston's dynamic perfectly when he watched the two play craps together and start arguing over which one should throw. Louis settled it by grabbing the dice and saying, "I'm the idol around here."

The men understood each other with the fine antennae of country boys who, at the heights of their careers, were still regarded as dumb black men. A *Washington Post* columnist once quoted Louis talking as if he were Uncle Remus, saying, "Ah din't uh pick'in no spots. I sure do wish I could g'home and tak a leetle nap. I ain't had no sleep in almost an hour now . . ."

They also had similar appetites for gambling and women, although Louis's tastes ran to the higher end. He lent his name to everything from soda cans to cigarettes so he could pay off the debts he'd run up putting a thousand bucks on holes of golf and bedding starlets. (He was rumored to have had affairs with Eartha Kitt and Jayne Mansfield.)

The relationship wasn't entirely one-sided. When Joe was losing his shirt promoting fights in Los Angeles early in the sixties, Sonny took time out of his schedule to make an appearance, helping to put a few thousand bucks in his friend's pocket. And when he went to Vegas in 1963 to get ready for his rematch with Patterson, he gave Louis a job in his entourage.

But there was no escaping the fact that Joe had done what Sonny couldn't, which was let white America adopt him as its own. Seventy million people listened on the radio when Louis met Max Schmeling for the second time in 1938 and battered the German so mercilessly that his cornerman finally threw a white towel into the ring. Writing in *The New York Times*, James P. Dawson observed: "It was as if [Schmeling] had been poleaxed. His brain was awhirl, his body, his head, his jaws ached and pained, his senses were numbed from that furious, paralyzing punching he had taken even in the short space of time the battle consumed."

Black America was delirious with the win. "There never was

a Harlem like the Harlem of Wednesday night," wrote the *Daily Worker.* "Take a dozen Harlem Christmases, a score of New Year's Eves, a bushel of July 4ths and maybe—yes, maybe—you get a faint glimpse of the idea." In later years, veterans of all colors treated Louis with reverence, often remembering the day they signed up to serve and saw the poster of him at the U.S. Army recruitment center, dressed in uniform and lunging forward with a bayonet. That was the image they clung to, and not the one that Red Smith chronicled in the *New York Herald Tribune* after Louis's last fight in 1951 with Rocky Marciano, when he wrote: "Memory retains scores of pictures of Joe in his dressing room, always sitting up, relaxed, answering questions in his slow, thoughtful way. This time only, he was down."

If Smith could have traveled ahead to Las Vegas in 1969 and seen the life Louis made with his third wife, Martha, a successful Los Angeles trial attorney, he would have seen a man who'd discovered the pleasures of buffets, jogging suits, and the desert air. "I hear people say how the casinos took advantage of Joe, but that's bullshit," his close friend, Gene Kilroy, told me in an interview. "He could take two people or twenty people out to dinner without paying a dime. He loved it. Vegas was a new world for him."

Heroin was just another thing that Joe did longer and better than Sonny. He started using in the early sixties and for most of the decade managed to hide his habit behind that big, gregarious smile. But it became harder to pretend everything was just fine. Martha noticed the change in late 1969, when Joe began acting strangely in their apartment in Los Angeles. First he started taping up the electrical outlets because he was afraid that poison gas might leak in. Then he moved their bed to the dresser and built a cocoon out of furniture and window shades so he could climb inside it fully clothed in the hopes of curing his insomnia. As Martha told Joe's biographer Barney Nagler, "It was the most pathetic thing in the world."

She hoped whatever it was would stop on its own. But it didn't. In January 1970 they went to Tuscaloosa to see Jesse Owens, another good friend, get inducted into the Alabama Sports Hall of Fame. When Owens stopped by their room, he found Joe detaching an air-conditioning vent and mumbling, "I ain't scared. I'm Joe Louis, heavyweight champion of the world." The next month, while the couple was in Miami on business, Martha caught her husband smearing mayonnaise into imaginary cracks in the smooth ceiling, trying to stop the gas that he was sure was leaking through.

And then there was the sleep. Joe couldn't fall asleep at night because he was convinced that a sinister character he called "The Texan" was following him. By late spring, his mind was so bent that Martha begged him to see a doctor they knew in Detroit. But as Louis would later write in his autobiography, *My Life*:

> He told me I should go to a hospital. At first I agreed with him and said yes. Then I thought to myself, if I agree with him, I'm saying something's wrong with me. So I cut out of there. . . . I went to all the secret places I knew about in the country. . . . What was wrong with me? I didn't know. All I knew was that I wanted to keep

moving. I stayed in some odd places with people who didn't want any publicity so nothing got in the papers and I kept hidden from America for a while.

Ash Resnick, for one, thought Louis was just being eccentric. "Joe was harmless, even though he had these hallucinations," Resnick told Nagler. "He wasn't hurting anybody. He was like a kid. He wanted to tape up the ventilators in his room and stuff up the cracks and open the windows wide, so what? He'd say don't turn on the television set, there's poison gas coming out of there. Those were things within himself."

Only when Louis's advancing dementia started to interfere with his work at Caesars did Resnick seem to take notice. "I got very much concerned one day in Las Vegas," he went on. "A friend of Joe's was playing blackjack. This guy was playing high stakes and Joe just stood near him, looking over his shoulder. Now, there was this other fellow standing behind Joe, looking at the game, an absolute stranger. All of a sudden Joe turned around to the guy and says, 'I know you're following me. You'd better get out of here. I'll knock you right on your ass.' . . . I really got concerned, you know, because I felt, God forbid, if any violence showed up in Joe, it was time to do something."

It's hard to overstate how dependent the two heavyweight champions were on each other. Lem Banker recalls them coming to his Sahara Health Club for long saunas and steams and laughing like high school kids. They went to fights together, shot craps together, ate sumptuous meals at Caesars' Bacchanal Room like Greek gods together.

But by late April of 1970 that friendship was breaking apart. Martha became so convinced that Joe needed professional help that she got him to take a spring vacation at their place in Denver without mentioning that she'd found out that Colorado allowed for involuntary commitments, and Joe's son, who was going to school there, agreed to sign the papers to commit him. On May 1 three sheriff's deputies and a probate officer showed up to the Louis home and patiently explained to Joe that they were there to take him to the Colorado Psychiatric Hospital for his own good. In his then state of mind, he concluded his only option was to reach for the phone and call Richard Nixon to let the president know he was about to be kidnapped. "Our biggest problem was convincing him that he needed help," Martha told reporters when word of his hospitalization leaked out. "And I'm still not sure he realizes that."

If Sonny needed to be reminded how deeply the public cared for Joe—and how little it seemed to care about Sonny himself— it came in August, when Motown's Berry Gordy threw an all-star televised "Salute to the Champ, Joe Louis" program at the Cobo Arena in Detroit to help the Louises pay their medical bills. Joe was supposed to make the trip but got scared at the last minute and stayed home, leaving Martha and his kids to sit front and center for a lineup that included the Jackson 5, B.B. King, and the Four Tops. Gordy asked Sonny to make a cameo with Redd Foxx, who was still playing Vegas, and when their time came they walked on with a canned shtick in which Foxx quipped that they were "a fox and a bear on the same show for the first time."

But even there, in Joe's darkest public hour, Sonny still was made to feel like the lesser man. *Ebony* magazine devoted a five-page pictorial to the benefit that was accompanied by a story about the so-called heavyweight jinx. It said, "When one looks at the heavyweight champions who followed Louis, it would not be difficult to become convinced that there must be a jinx on any black man who holds the title. . . . Sonny Liston, well into his 40s, is still trying to make it as a boxer."

Still trying to make it? Sonny must have thrown the magazine across the room when he saw that. His record was 50–4 and he'd been part of the four biggest title fights of the decade. He didn't need false praise. But shit, after all of that, was a little respect from those "educated Negroes" who were supposed to be his own people too much to ask?

John Sutton drove into Las Vegas from Los Angeles in a two-tone blue Buick Electra 225 with mirrored rims and a horn that blared "La Cucaracha." It was one of the sweetest cars he'd ever laid his eyes on, and from the moment Sutton saw it at the LAPD's impound lot, he knew they were made for each other.

It was standard procedure for a visiting agent to announce himself to local law enforcement, but in this case Sutton went it alone because he wasn't sure who to trust. A recent front-page story in the *Sun* announced, "Top-level federal authorities have decided Las Vegas isn't any place to investigate organized crime." In ripping the curtain off a botched grand jury investigation of mobsters, the paper quoted a federal source as saying that clashes among the local cops, judges, strike force agents, and U.S. Department of Justice officials had paralyzed law enforcement. "We could not get a case through the courts in Las Vegas," the source told the paper.

Well, Sutton figured, if the shit hit the fan, he could always call the BNDD's station chief in Las Vegas to bail him out. But he wasn't planning on letting that happen. Notwithstanding the flamboyant ride, he wanted to keep a low profile, and he chose a hotel, the Villa Roma, that was a few blocks off the Strip and just far away enough from the action to suit his purposes.

Once he unpacked his things, he opened a briefcase full of files. There were assorted locations he'd been asked to check out and a couple of sources to meet. The bureau was also interested in a network of blackjack dealers who were taking orders at the big hotels and passing them to couriers for door-to-door delivery. But most of all he looked forward to making headway with the Sonny Liston file that had been sitting on his desk for weeks.

Looking into the mirror, he checked out his appearance. He'd bought himself an ankle-length leather coat, a wide brimmed hat, and fake diamond rings that drew attention to his almost impossibly thick fingers. Satisfied that he looked "fly," he set off to try his luck on the Strip.

First he tried Caesars. Then he hit the Sahara. Finally he wound his way to the Riviera. At each stop he'd get a drink, nurse it, and then case the casino before he settled on a blackjack dealer to approach. These were cold hits, meaning nothing had been set up, so he played up his act, sidling up to the tables as a gangster and striking up conversations. At some point he'd slip in a casual drug reference, something along the lines of "Who's got it?" that was supposed to mean "Who's holding dope?"

He hadn't had any luck by the end of the last evening, when his last stop was the Union Plaza hotel, a kitschy landmark that overlooked the heart of Glitter Gulch. Sutton did his usual act, but this time he felt a pair of eyes following him as he canvassed the room. Deciding to cut his losses, he left the hotel and bundled himself back into the Electra, when he saw a guy jotting down his license plate.

Sutton kept his cool and drove back to his hotel, so exhausted that he didn't even remember climbing into bed before he was asleep. He was awoken at dawn by the room phone. Who the hell? Nobody had his number.

He grabbed for the receiver to hear the voice of the BNDD's station chief in Vegas, Dick Robinson. "You've been made," Robinson said.

Sutton cleared the cobwebs from his head to figure out what the hell he was talking about. Then he remembered the guy from the night before. The one scribbling the number of his license plate.

"Who?" he asked.

"One of ours," Robinson replied. "You're lucky."

A BNDD informant had noticed him at the Riviera and figured he was a new player in town.

The agents managed to have a laugh over the episode. But it

meant that Sutton would have to cut his work short on this trip. If one informant had made him, there was a pretty good chance another one might have as well.

Sutton would regroup and make a run at Sonny on his next visit, when he'd be sure to be less conspicuous.

9.

"BETTER WAKE VIC DAMONE"

On Tuesday morning, September 1, 1970, with the weather forecast calling for an afternoon high of 105 degrees, the polls opened for the residents of Clark County to vote in primary elections. In predicting that 70 percent of the county's 87,778 registered voters would cast their ballots, the *Sun* noted, "The issue which has drawn the most fire and public interest appears to be the quality of law enforcement in Clark County."

Recently released statistics from the FBI's annual crime report that showed Nevada had the third-highest overall crime rate in the nation. When it came to property crimes, only California, with 3,642 per 100,000 residents, exceeded Nevada's average. The news wasn't much better with respect to murder, rape, and manslaughter. Nevada was a bloody ninth in the nation. (Four decades later, it would be up to second.)

President Nixon was so afraid of losing control of a state that he carried by only 12,590 votes in 1968 that he sent his vice president, Spiro Agnew, to headline a GOP fund-raiser at the Sahara Hotel for 1,500 tuxedoed guests who paid $100 each. Agnew came to blame drugs for Nevada's problems and he wasted no time taking aim at the liberals, who he accused of creating a "psychedelic Tin Pan Alley."

In what must have seemed like a particularly effective generational reference, the vice president cited the Beatles song "With a Little Help from My Friends" and its lyrics—"I get by with a little help from my friends, I get high with a little help from my friends." Leaning into his microphone, he told his audience that he'd learned on good authority the "friends" in the lyrics referred to "Mary Jane," "Benny," and "Speed."

The man who popularized the phrase "nattering nabobs of negativism" went on to attack the "pornographic peddling producers [who are] still succumbing to the temptation of the sensational, and playing right into the hands of the drug culture." Then, nailing the line he'd been sent by Nixon to deliver, Agnew pounded his fist and concluded the only way to turn back the tide was by voting Republican. "That is how the drug culture will be defeated. That is how the character of the American people, in its dignity and fierce individuality, will triumph again!"

(Agnew didn't mention William Campbell, a parking lot attendant who was running for sheriff against John Sleeper and Ralph Lamb on the single issue of legalizing marijuana. With

THE MURDER OF SONNY LISTON

the election just days away, a grand jury indicted Campbell for dealing thirteen kilos, leading to a surreal scene in which sheriff's deputies showed up at his home to serve an arrest warrant and found him holding a shotgun and threatening to kill the men he'd hoped to lead.)

Crooks are practical people, and Red Rodney and Earl Cage—even Ash Resnick, whose gambling activities remained the subject of a continuing investigation by the FBI—all understood that this was a good time to lay low. Drugs and gambling had become third-rail issues and no one wanted to be electrified by them. Their hope was that, once the election passed, things would return to normal.

But at the moment nothing was normal on the campaign trail. John Sleeper was hitting Sheriff Lamb at every turn, ratcheting up his accusations that Clark County's deputies were taking protection money to let dealers roam free. In a debate a few days earlier, he'd stared into the camera and darkly warned that Las Vegas couldn't survive four more years of Ralph Lamb's corrupt brand of cowboy justice.* Behind the scenes, however, the Sleeper campaign was in the process of self-destructing. When it came time for the candidate to prove his charges, he showed up in front of a grand jury strangely empty-handed.

"I remember testifying for one of the officers he accused, a good man," Dick Robinson, the Vegas station chief for the

---

*In 1977, Lamb faced tax evasion charges after IRS agents alleged he didn't report more than $79,000 of earnings between 1970 and 1972. That case ultimately was dismissed, but four years later federal prosecutors unsealed a 1978 recording of the New Jersey mobster Anthony Russo bragging that he had paid Lamb $100 a month.

BNDD, told me. "I don't know what it was, but Sleeper just seemed to hate other cops." By the same token, he didn't seem to be shy about using his office to benefit himself. When a casino executive refused to give Sleeper a campaign contribution, he mysteriously found himself the subject of a raid by city narcs who hauled away his customers on marijuana and prostitution charges. On the eve of the primary, the *Sun*'s widely read political columnist Paul Price warned his readers that Sleeper was "not personally, professionally or emotionally qualified to be Sheriff of Clark County."

The one ace that Sleeper felt he still had up his sleeve, however, was the city's African-American community. A survey done for *Time* magazine showed that the rhetoric of groups like the Black Panther Party was catching on. A Harris survey found that "two out of every three white people in the United States feel that the 'Black Panthers are a serious menace to the country.'" Yet fully a quarter of the 1,255 African-Americas who were surveyed called the group's philosophy "the same as mine." Among black teenagers that number skyrocketed to 43 percent. So it was not surprising that the biggest racial flashpoint in Las Vegas was in the city's schools.

The largest and most diverse of Clark County's seven high schools was Rancho High. On the far north side of the city, it drew its students from a cross section of working-class neighborhoods that included blacks, Hispanics, and Native Americans. (A small reservation was carved out nearby.) These were the children of the cooks and janitors and mechanics who kept the Strip running and who lived under a hierarchal kind of harmony. As a student from the class of 1971 would recall in a documentary about the riots by the Las Vegas filmmaker Stan Armstrong: "The word 'nigger' really wasn't in my opinion . . . a racial term. It was just what a black person was." Added another: "I was prejudiced for a long time. But I was never a racist."

In that atmosphere, something as simple as a walk to school became a test of wills. The dividing line was the bridge that ran over the Union Pacific Railroad tracks on Owens Avenue. "We called it Vegas Village Hill," says Armstrong, who graduated from Rancho in 1972. "A lot of times when you'd cross on the way to school, you were subject to white kids throwing rocks at you and calling you the N-word."

On the morning of May 20, word started to spread through the hallways that there was going to be a war at the snack bar that afternoon. Somehow no one in the school's administration learned about the plan until more than three hundred students showed up to face off against one another. It didn't matter who threw the first punch. They all knew what they were there for and got down to it fast. At three minutes past one, the school was a scene of flying fists, pipes, and weapons that had been hidden for just such a purpose. With the riots of the prior fall still fresh in everyone's mind, a call went out for all available cops to come to the scene. A half hour after the first punch was thrown, seventy members of the North Las Vegas PD, the Sheriff's Department, and the Highway Patrol showed up in riot gear and toting water cannons to literally cool the students down.

Had things ended there, with the cops hosing them into small clusters, the episode might not have been viewed as an example of excessive force. But it didn't end there. While eight teens were brought to the hospital, one with a fractured jaw, white students were given court appearance tickets and sent home on their own. The blacks, by contrast, were manhandled onto school buses and those who resisted were sprayed with Mace and shoved into seats while they begged for medical help that never arrived.

When angry parents demanded an explanation, the North Las Vegas chief of police insisted that using Mace was more humane than clubs or nightsticks. But it was hard to counter the black-owned *Las Vegas Voice* when it argued, "The community must have assurances that our law enforcement officers will not get *mace happy*."

The next morning, a cordon of police surrounded the school, giving it the same feel as college campuses that were being riven by protests over the Vietnam War. In a show of defiance, several dozen students made their way to the school's library, where they staged a sit-in and refused the principal's order to go to class. As described by the *Las Vegas Review-Journal*, "Some were reported singing and banging books around." Eventually, the cops got fifty of them on a bus and dropped them off at Juvenile Hall, where they were all booked on loitering charges.

It was not a promising way to begin a summer that promised to be full of racial tension and strife. As the months wore on, the *Voice* kept its readers apprised of the racial progress being made elsewhere. In July, California's supreme court allowed a black truck driver, Manuel Alcorn, to sue his bosses for calling him a "nigger," ruling that:

The term may once have been common usage, along with other racial characterizations as "Wop," "Chink," "Jap," "bohunk" and "shanty Irish." But [it] has become particularly abusive and insulting in light of recent developments in the civil rights movement as it pertains to the American Negro.

Still, change was slow. A Harris survey from the same period found that "on nearly every count a clear majority of white people simply have no contact on any level with Negroes." At most, 32 percent reported having contact with blacks where they worked. Even more eye opening, 88 percent said they had "no black friends they see socially or no black neighbors."

Once the *Review-Journal* drilled down into its high schools, it found the divisions were even more alarming. "Whites try to impress on us that we're second class citizens," one African-American girl told the paper. "They tell us, 'You can come to work and school, but then you go back to your own part of the city.'" Another remarked, "I've heard comments from Mormon students like, 'I'm not supposed to talk to you because we're taught that blacks don't exist.'"

It was little wonder, then, that the election for sheriff dominated the talk in African-American barbershops and church pews. The problem for Sleeper was that for every poster he hammered into a yard, Ralph Lamb had thousands of dollars to spend on television ads. For every VFW hall that he visited to warn about corruption in the sheriff's ranks, Lamb had a black-tie event where attendees could laud his stellar record on crime. Most important, the sheriff had the power of incumbency to show off the long arm of his law. With the election barely a week away, he hauled in a pair of fugitives who were wanted for bludgeoning to death a motel owner in a grisly crime five years earlier.

The message was clear: Las Vegas was Ralph Lamb's town, and if he wanted you, there was nowhere to hide. That's one reason why Sonny would have kept his drug dealing confined to the Westside. Since it was under the control of the friendlier Las Vegas PD, he had the freedom to do pretty much what he wanted there. Almost anywhere else would have been in Lamb's jurisdiction, which was something he would have wanted to avoid. In fact, if Sonny needed an example of how petulant Lamb could be, he only had to watch what was happening to the one celebrity who should have been truly untouchable.

A s the Labor Day 1970 weekend neared, the marquees along the Strip filled up with the biggest names in entertainment. Dionne Warwick was at the Sands. The Supremes and George Carlin were at the Frontier. Ike & Tina Turner were playing with Redd Foxx in the International's theater, while Elvis was finishing his marathon run in the showroom. Joan Rivers was at the Riviera.

But no name was bigger than Frank. After the dissolution of the Rat Pack in 1966, Sinatra released *Sinatra at the Sands*, with Count Basie and His Orchestra, to reviews that were lavish. The owners of the resort were so thrilled that they gave him a house account for a gambling habit that often saw him lose tens of thousands on blackjack. The party at the Sands ended in 1967 when Howard Hughes arrived in town and bought the hotel. Hughes was bitter at Sinatra for stealing away the actress Ava Gardner and eager to settle an old score, and he capped Sinatra's house account at a measly $3,000. Paul Anka was at the singer's side when he learned about the move. He recalled Sinatra "yelling and screaming right in the middle of the casino" as he stood on top of a craps table. When he wouldn't calm down, Carl Cohen, the hotel's vice president and a former boxer, punched him in the mouth.

After that, Sinatra moved across the street to Caesars and he'd been playing there every year since. The hotel's staff hated him. In particular, they couldn't get over an incident where he held out one of his feet to trip a busboy and then flicked a hundred-dollar casino chip at the kid for laughs while trays were splattered all over the floor. The management, however, was thrilled to have the biggest name in town and gave him a deal that was commensurate. Unlike Elvis, who needed amphetamines to get through two shows a night every night,* Sinatra had to perform only twice on Wednesdays and Saturdays. Otherwise, he performed a single show at 10:30 p.m. with a day off on Sunday. The casino's management rolled out an ad for him that read, "When the man sings, he is ten feet tall. He is a pure thoroughbred . . ."

---

*According to Jeff Burbank's book *Las Vegas Babylon: True Tales of Glitter, Glamour, and Greed,* the pharmacy in Hughes's Landmark Hotel across the street would rush orders to Elvis's door.

Four days into his 1970 run, however, Sinatra managed to find trouble again. After he'd finished the second of his Saturday shows, he was at the baccarat table when he tried raising the stakes on an already high-stakes game. The owners of Caesars weren't as stingy as those at the Sands, but they still had their limits, and the casino's manager, Sanford "Sandy" Waterman, went out to explain that they couldn't stake Sinatra another $16,000.

Small details vary, but most witnesses agreed that Sinatra hurled a handful of chips at the sixty-six-year-old and the two got into a tussle. Waterman slammed a door on Sinatra's arm, leading Sinatra to pry it loose and coldcock him with his good arm. With bystanders trying to pull them apart, Waterman took out a .38 and pointed it at Sinatra. Lunging for Waterman's throat, Sinatra shouted something like "I hope you like that gun because you may have to eat it." Twenty-four hours later, he was leaving town with the parting advice "Better wake Vic Damone."

The city's district attorney, George Franklin, was quick to absolve Waterman. "My reports indicate he still had finger marks on his throat from where Sinatra grabbed him," the DA told the press. "There seems to be reasonable grounds for making the assumption that Sinatra was the aggressor all the way." When reached for comment at his home in Los Angeles, Sinatra played the victim. "If the public officials who seek newspaper exposure by harassing me and other entertainers don't get off my back," he said, "it is of little moment to me if I ever play Las Vegas again."

But Sinatra underestimated Lamb's single-mindedness. In a muscular move, the cowboy sheriff ordered Sinatra back to town to give a statement in the matter. He also warned that if Sinatra wanted to play on the Strip again, he'd have to apply for a work card just like the Beatles. "If he gives me any trouble," Lamb threw in, "he's going to jail."

Yes, Las Vegas was Ralph Lamb's town.

On primary day, fewer than one-third of the expected voters showed up to hand their sheriff reelection with a commanding 5,338-vote margin out of 18,756 votes cast.* Lamb was gracious, calling the win "a tremendous vote of confidence, not only for me personally but also for my officers." But if the results suggested anything, it was that the residents of Las Vegas liked having a father figure who knew how to keep the party from getting too out of hand.

John Sleeper, meanwhile, was noticeably silent. He returned to his day-shift detective desk at the police department without any of his usual bravado. He'd gambled and lost, and if Las Vegas had been Sicily, he would have been expected to go home and slice his own wrists. But since it wasn't, the smart move would

---

*In another seven years, a federal grand jury would indict Lamb on tax evasion charges for failing to report $30,000 in gifts given to him by a casino mogul, later calling it a loan. But even then Lamb seemed to be bulletproof. In acquitting but not actually clearing the sheriff, a federal judge rendered the opinion that "many fringe benefits come to a public official which may be accepted along with the honest discharge of duties." Corruption, in other words, was in the eye of the beholder.

have been for him to take some time off to reassess his career. After all, he'd gone from commanding a battalion of swashbuckling undercover officers to a desk job with uncertain prospects.

Instead, Sleeper doubled down in a move that was both dangerous and foolhardy. Marshaling all of the claims he couldn't prove during the campaign, he wrote a long letter to the Justice Department in Washington, D.C., demanding that the feds launch a full-scale investigation into Lamb's political machine. An article that appeared in the *Sun* reported:

> Police Lt. John Sleeper lost his bid for sheriff of Clark County but apparently he is still trying to make his voice heard. He wrote a letter shortly after the election to the federal task force on crime in Washington. His letter was referred to the L.A. office, where last week he was contacted by a member of this task force. Reportedly, Sleeper's letter tells the task force about wrongdoings by both police officers and deputies. And about a political machine that caused his defeat in the September primary election.

It's worth pausing again to consider how much paranoia was raging through a very small world. Thanks to Sleeper, a federal task force was looking into whether Lamb and his officers took payoffs to let heroin dealers off the hook. In the meantime the city's district attorney was conducting a separate investigation into whether Sleeper had perjured himself before a grand jury that jettisoned his claims. Apart from that, John Sutton, the federal drug agent, was working on city and county turf without telling the sheriff or police chief, because he didn't know whom he could trust. And the FBI was crawling all over the Strip, listening to those six hundred wiretaps and looking to make cases.

If you were a crook, this was bad for business. It was hard to figure out who to pay off and who to stay away from. But it was even more dangerous for informants who had to choose sides. It was a bad time . . . a really bad time . . . to get careless.

10.

—

ATLANTA

While Clark County voters were going to the polls on September 1, Muhammad Ali left his home in Philadelphia to fly to Atlanta for what he hoped would be a new beginning.

After defending his title against Liston in 1965, Ali had fought eight more times. But it was his politics, not his pugilism, that he was becoming known for best. On a swing through Europe in 1966, he declared that he would no longer answer to the name Cassius Clay and announced he did not care to sleep with white women because for "black to be beautiful," it couldn't be diluted by white blood. In a 1966 *Chicago Tribune* profile headlined "Champion Changes from Hero to Bum in Six Years," reporter Robert Markus asked what had happened to the most popular American at the Rome Olympics in 1960. "What happened in the intervening years to turn Cassius Clay . . . into a renegade, despised by his countrymen?"

And all of this was before Ali received the April 28, 1967, notice inducting him into the armed services.

It wasn't the first draft notice Ali had gotten. He had received one in 1963, too, but he showed up for his medical exam acting so crazy that he got classified as 1-Y, which meant he was qualified only in the event of a war or national emergency. Still, as his star continued to climb, the draft board kept an eye on him, and in 1967 he suddenly found himself bumped up to 1-A, which made him immediately eligible to serve. "How could they do this to the champion?" he asked. "The taxes from my fights alone pay salaries for 200,000 soldiers a year."

Ali could easily have done what Joe Louis did in World War II and become a celebrity soldier, fighting exhibitions to entertain the troops. The Army might have even let him fight a real title bout or two. But he wanted none of it. His lawyers filed for an exemption, first arguing hardship, then that the war violated his beliefs as a Muslim minister. After a four-fight swing though Toronto, London, and Germany, Ali returned home to find that the U.S. Justice Department, wary of recognizing the Nation of Islam and eager to make an example of him, was preparing to charge him with violating the Military Selective Service Act.

At a news conference in which he announced he had no intention of serving in Vietnam, Ali vowed that his "conscience won't let me go shoot my brother, or some darker people, or some poor hungry people in the mud for big powerful America.

And shoot them for what? They never called me nigger. They never lynched me. They didn't put no dogs on me. They didn't rob me of my nationality, rape and kill my mother and father. Shoot them for what? How am I going to shoot them . . . little babies and children, women? How can I shoot them poor people? Just take me to jail."

On June 20, 1967, a federal jury voted to do just that. But the U.S. attorney in Houston, Morton Susman, tried to soften the blow by arguing for leniency. He reminded the judge that the defendant, who came dressed in a silk suit and alligator shoes, was an Olympic hero who'd only adopted his Muslim faith after defeating Liston for the title. "In my opinion . . . this tragedy and the loss of his title could be traced to that," Susman said, adding that justice would be served if Ali received less than the five-year maximum sentence. But they were in Texas and the judge, not persuaded, gave him the five years.

While Ali's lawyers appealed his conviction, the fighter stayed in the public eye, lecturing on college campuses, where his message of religious pacifism played to students of all colors, and starring in a short-lived black power musical on Broadway. He was at his most fiery, though, when he sat down for an interview with a new magazine, *The Black Scholar*. "I'm supposed to be . . . walking around somewhere broke," he began, taunting those who expected a more chastened tone. "But I surprised them; I'm doing better. . . . I'm not depending on the white power structure and that boxing game for survival. . . . Fighters are just brutes that come to entertain the rich. Beat up on each other and break each other's noses, show off like two little monkeys for the crowd, killing each other for the crowd. And half of the crowd is white. We're slaves in that ring." In an echo of the walks he took through Las Vegas's Westside with Wilbur Jackson, he lamented "the tragedy of the life of the black man today" and exhorted the magazine's readers to "go on and join something. If it isn't the Muslims, at least join the Black Panthers."

Whether Ali's disavowal of boxing was an honest reflection of his faith or a shrewd way to make himself more valuable remained to be seen. But it had its intended effect. *The Ring* magazine published a weighty cover story that announced it was abandoning its three-year campaign to keep Ali recognized as the heavyweight champion. It was hard to argue with the choice of Joe Frazier as "Clay's legal and indisputable successor to the title." He'd fought the fight of his life against the other contender for Ali's vacated WBA title, the Kentuckian Jimmy Ellis, at Madison Square Garden. As *The Ring*'s publisher, Nat Fleischer, wrote: "If, as many skeptics predict, Clay changes his mind about quitting the ring and the lush paydays which would become available to him if he were cleared by the Supreme Court, Cassius would have to appear as the challenger and emphatically not as the champion."

As a result of the declaration, *The Ring* rewrote its rankings in this order:

World Champion: Joe Frazier, Philadelphia, Pa.
1. Leotis Martin, Philadelphia, Pa.
2. Jimmy Ellis, Louisville, Ky.
3. Mac Foster, Fresno, Calif.

THE MURDER OF SONNY LISTON

4. Oscar Bonavena, Argentina

5. Sonny Liston, Las Vegas, Nev.

Behind the scenes, though, Ali was pressing his managers to get him back into the ring. Three years without a steady means of support was a long time, and all the campus lectures in the world couldn't replace the payday of a title fight. Ali made the mistake of admitting as much to Howard Cosell in April 1969 when he said he hoped to return to boxing to pay off his debts. His candor earned a sharp rebuke from Elijah Muhammad, who issued a statement saying, "We, the Muslims, are not with Mr. Muhammad Ali, in his desire to work in the sports world for the sake of a 'leetle' money." To get back into the Prophet's good graces and end the yearlong suspension that prevented him from talking to other Muslims, Ali told *The Black Scholar* that he deserved the punishment for doubting "that my God and what I believe can't take care of me."

Ali's managers arranged exhibitions everywhere from a bullring in Tijuana to a rodeo park in an all-black community in Tulsa. But as soon as a deal looked imminent, something went wrong. Florida's governor, Claude Kirk, seemed happy to let Ali come to Tampa until the *Tribune*'s editorial writers stirred up their readers by announcing, "We object conscientiously." Nevada's governor, Paul Laxalt, reportedly signed off on a deal for Ali to fight in Las Vegas until Howard Hughes raised bloody hell on the grounds that it was both immoral and unpatriotic to aid Ali's return. Ali went as far as agreeing to a twenty-four-hour trip to Toronto to fight Frazier in which he would post a

$100,000 bond and be escorted by U.S. marshals. But a federal judge torpedoed the deal.

Ali thought he was close when the city council in Charleston, South Carolina, voted to let him hold a charity benefit in their city. Even ABC's *Wide World of Sports* signed on to cover it. But that, too, fell apart when the state's powerful Democratic congressman, L. Mendel Rivers, the chairman of the Armed Services Committee, balked at celebrating a draft dodger and pressured the council to withdraw its approval.

"We were coming down here to help these black youths learn boxing," Ali said before boarding his flight home. "But all this scufflin' has been humiliating and insulting. I don't want to bother anybody so I'm leaving."*

L eroy Johnson hadn't followed these developments closely. The first African-American to get elected to Georgia's state legislature in nearly a century really wasn't much of a sports fan. But he was politically wired. And when one of Ali's interlocutors reached out to him through a mutual friend, seeking any influence he could wield to get a fight held in Atlanta, Johnson discovered that Georgia was different from the other states where Ali had been denied in one key respect: it didn't have a state athletic commission. Instead, fights were the purview of local

---

* Barrett tried to switch the site to the Charlotte Speedway, but Ali balked at being so exposed. "I ain't getting out here in any ring and letting a bunch of rednecks shoot me like they did Martin Luther King," he said, according to Michael Arkush in the book *The Fight of the Century: Ali vs. Frazier, March 8, 1971.*

authorities. That meant that the board of aldermen would be in charge of issuing licenses in Atlanta.

That was remarkably good news for Ali, since Johnson's influence on the board ran deep. In a matter of a few weeks, he met with all the important politicians in his state to soften the ground, making the case that times were changing and Atlanta could be in the vanguard of a New South. By licensing Ali, the city could make a statement about its people and their commitment to progressive politics.

It was a canny, constructive argument. When Johnson finished making his rounds, he'd done what none of the politically connected promoters who'd worked for Ali had succeeded in doing: he'd gotten him a license to fight.

Ali was skeptical when Johnson asked him to come to Atlanta for an introductory press conference. After what he'd already been through, he didn't want to be embarrassed again. But Johnson insisted that this wouldn't be a repeat. They had the backing of the city, no matter what any court said about his draft case. Even so, Ali arrived at the Atlanta Municipal Airport in a subdued mood. Johnson and a white businessman named Harry Pett were there to meet him, and when Pett was asked why Atlanta didn't seem to be roiled by the same protests that followed Ali elsewhere, he beamed and said, "Atlanta is too busy to hate. It's the finest city in the world."

From the airport, Ali was driven to a Marriott downtown where reporters were gathering for a press conference. They weren't told that he was in the building, and he went to one of the upstairs rooms, where a speakerphone was set up for him to listen in on the proceedings. Promoter Robert Kassel led the event, and as he teased out the drama, Ali waited . . . and waited . . . for what everyone had come to hear: that the board of aldermen had issued a license. Atlanta was welcoming the champ back.

Or, at least, kind of back. For his first public event, Kassel arranged for Ali to get eight rounds of practice against three unheralded heavyweights in the gym of Morehouse College. Noting the sentimental irony of the choice, *Jet* magazine observed: "Morehouse is the site where Dr. Martin Luther King, Jr., was buried and now it is a place where Ali is resurrected."

The fans who filled the gym the next evening were as curious as Ali to see what he had left. All the puttering that he'd been doing around his house in Cherry Hill, New Jersey, had added twenty-five pounds to his former fighting weight, and his coal-fired eyes were buried under puffy cheeks. "I'm just as anxious as anybody to see what I can do," he told reporters. "I think this will tell me just how off I am."

Writing in *The Ring*, Joe Louis's former trainer, Mannie Seamon, sounded a skeptical note, writing that "Clay was a fine fighter in his time. But take him out of the field in which he won and defended the heavyweight championship and he has to be flawed. To begin with, Cassius needed a big ring in which to make his mobility count most. He needed a ring with a lot of padding. He required a ring with tight ropes." Recalling his first fight with Sonny, Seamon observed, "Clay had some serious flaws in his style and method. But in his time and against this field, these flaws did not show up to cost him in any way. A great fighter has to observe certain laws of leverage and balance. Clay won despite ignoring this, in some cases to a great extent."

The new-model Ali wasn't any humbler than the old one. Although the gym in Atlanta trapped every last degree of the Georgia summer heat, he entered it as if he were floating on ice. Wearing a short white robe, he coolly waved to a crowd that included Martin Luther King Sr. and his family, then threw off the robe and got down to business. His first opponent, Rufus Brassell, a career sparring partner, seemed happy that his assignment was merely to last two rounds, long enough for the ex-champ to test out a couple of jabs and a swift one-two combo. In another two-rounder, Ali threw a few punches at the Miami heavyweight Johnny Hudgins. But as *Sports Illustrated* writer Martin Kane observed, "It disappointed the crowd that Ali was giving them so little action, and at the end of the first round of his four-rounder against George Hill there were scattered boos." Eager to see if he could punch himself out of trouble, Ali let himself get cornered in the second round, then unleashed a fifteen-second flurry of punches in the third, and finally, in the fourth, unveiled the fan-pleasing Ali shuffle before attacking Hill's body and head.

In the dressing room afterward, Ali sat naked and sweating because of the sweltering heat. Asked to sum up his performance, he said what was obvious to everyone, including Joe Frazier. "I'm not in condition for Frazier yet," he said.

O nce Atlanta's board of aldermen saw that the city hadn't burned—or even kindled—as a result of Ali's exhibition, they fast-tracked their approval for him to fight Jerry Quarry at the Municipal Auditorium on October 26. The same day that fight was announced, Joe Frazier announced he was meeting Bob Foster, the light-heavyweight champ, in what everyone assumed would be his final stop before he claimed Ali.

But as much as Ali's camp was eager to see what he had in his tank, the real tune-up wasn't going to be in the ring. It was going to be with the closed-circuit technology that promised to turn any fight Ali might have with Frazier into the biggest cash cow in the history of sport.

As Michael Arkush notes in his book *The Fight of the Century*, the first closed-circuit broadcast in the history of boxing came on June 15, 1951, and featured a bout between Joe Louis, who was then thirty-seven, and Lee Savold, a journeyman Minnesotan on the downside of his career. Roughly twenty-two thousand fans in eight cities paid between fifty cents and $1.30 to see Louis win in six rounds.

A decade later, six hundred thousand fans paid a total of $4.5 million to see Liston knock out Floyd Patterson in the first round of their 1962 fight. A couple of years later they plunked down $4 million to see him fight Ali in Miami, which was particularly impressive, since the oddsmakers were predicting a walkover.

Sonny saw barely a dime of that money. He left Chicago so

poor after the feds impounded his gate for fear it would go to the mob that an infamous photo was taken showing him pretending to hitch a ride out of town. In Miami, the IRS impounded another $2.7 million of his closed-circuit revenue, arguing that his Intercontinental Promotions owed at least that much in back taxes.

Ali, by contrast, was coming back at the precise moment that closed-circuit television was about to explode. In the moments before he got into the ring, an intern at Atlanta's Municipal Auditorium asked him what he was thinking. As recorded by George Plimpton, Ali said "he was thinking about the people in Japan and Turkey and Russia, all over the world; how they were beginning to think about the fight and about him; and the television sets being clicked on; and the traffic jams in front of the closed-circuit theaters; and how the big TV trucks out in back of the Atlanta arena, just by the stage door, were getting their machinery warmed up to send his image by satellite to all those people, and how he was going to dance for them."

His fight against Quarry would draw only five thousand fans to the Municipal Auditorium, but it was booked in two hundred theaters nationwide. If he could draw those kinds of numbers with a pair of tune-ups, promoters everywhere were salivating at what a fight with Frazier could do.

But as much as the press was looking toward that matchup, Ali's camp was focused on the still-dangerous Quarry. Three years younger than the twenty-eight-year-old Ali, and the youngest fighter Ali had ever faced professionally, Quarry had nearly won the heavyweight title twice, coming up just short to Jimmy

Ellis in the WBA's elimination tournament (the one that re-assigned Ali's title) and going seven brutal rounds against Joe Frazier. Ali's camp was respectful enough of Quarry to write a rematch clause into the deal in case he came up short. But publicly Ali was his usual dismissive self, telling reporters, "Don't forget, he ain't never fought the fastest heavyweight in history."

With only six weeks to prepare, Ali hunkered down with Angelo Dundee at the 5th St. Gym in Miami. Dundee wasn't unhappy with what he had to work with after the exhibition. Ali might still have been overweight, but his reflexes were intact and he was ready to run. After just a couple of weeks, visitors were stunned to see that he'd dropped two pants sizes and could now knot his necktie through his belt loops. By the weigh-in, Ali was all the way down to 213½, just three pounds more than when he'd fought Sonny in 1964.

On the evening of October 26, Atlanta was buzzing with energy. Men arrived in ankle-length fur coats while their dates wore pearls and, as former NAACP chairman Julian Bond later joked, "not much else." George Plimpton, who got sent to cover the fight for *The New Yorker*, wrote that he'd "never seen crowds as fancy, especially the men—felt headbands and feathered capes, and the stilted shoes, the heels like polished ebony, and many smoking stuff in odd meerschaum pipes."

(Not all the visitors to the city were so dignified. A gang of hoods who sold tickets to a fight-watching party looted their visitors when they arrived, before throwing them into a pad-locked basement. One woman who screamed that she had nowhere to move among all the hostages was told, "Dammit, just get on top of somebody.")

But of all the people in the Municipal Auditorium, no one looked as impressive as Ali. The loose-limbed upstart from Louisville was gone. This version was more manly, more muscular, and, as far as the Californian Quarry was concerned, more menacing. While Ali was warming up in the dressing room, a member of Quarry's inner circle, Willie Ketchum, tried to break the tension by saying, "I won some money on you once. I bet fifty dollars at seven to one that you'd whup Sonny Liston." That pleased Ali, who replied, "We'll give them a good show tonight." On the way to the ring, he stopped by Quarry's dressing room to warn him, "You best be in good shape because if you whup me, you've whupped the greatest fighter in the whole wide world."

Still, Ali couldn't help having butterflies. From the moment that he bounded into the ring in a white robe that had his name embossed on the back in huge red letters, he looked jittery, as if only the sound of his glove compacting bone would calm him down.

At the opening bell, Quarry was the aggressor, leaning in as he tried to find his range. But Ali kept snapping his head back, half boxer, half vaudevillian, establishing a perimeter from which he could operate. His first punch was a lead right, and even though Quarry had trained to anticipate Ali's ten-inch range, its speed still surprised him. The more frustrated Quarry became with Ali's advantage, the more weapons Ali unveiled, from jabs to one-two combinations to a five-punch flurry midway through the first round that reddened Quarry's nose. It took Quarry two and a half minutes before he finally crept out from behind his gloves and connected with a cross.

In the second round, Quarry settled into his game plan, using his huge left hook to scrape at Ali's ring rust. And by the third he was able to force his increasingly winded opponent into the ropes and a clench. But Ali wasn't in the mood to rope-a-dope. Sensing the need to finish things fast, he unleashed a pistonlike left that opened the scar tissue above Quarry's left eye, causing blood to start seeping into it. With predatory precision, he flicked three more punches at the cut, each meeting less resistance than the last. Quarry managed to clear the blood away long enough to find Ali's ribs. But as referee Tony Perez watched Quarry's cornermen work over the wound at the break, he decided he'd seen enough.

Quarry was on his feet, ready to get back to business for the fourth round, when Perez waved him off and stopped the fight. "You can't do that!" Quarry yelled. But before he could mount more of a protest, Ali was on him, smothering him in an embrace. Quarry gently backed down, understanding that the $150,000 he'd been guaranteed, his best payday to date, was for this exact moment.

The next day, October 27, the president of the United States emerged from the White House under a baleful sky to make a trip to the downtown office of the Bureau of Narcotics and Dangerous Drugs. A table had been set up for him that included charts of recent drug seizures and bindles of heroin from those raids. With the stern-faced agents who had made the seizures flanking him, the president was handed a pen and signed into law the Comprehensive Drug Abuse Prevention and Control Act of 1970.

The bill allowed narcotics to be divided—or, in the parlance of the law, *scheduled*—into different classes. The most restrictive category was reserved for drugs that had high potential for abuse and no accepted medical uses. Heroin was at the top of the list.

"The message that drugs can ruin young lives should be stressed in every home, every school, every church," Nixon said to a roomful of reporters.

Nixon's hope was that the new law would help him carry a tough law-and-order state like Nevada. But the state's top Republicans were worried enough about a political Waterloo that they begged the president to sell his domestic drug war in person.

On Halloween, a thousand mostly white Republicans turned out to welcome Nixon when he landed in *Air Force One* at Mc-Carran Airport. The evening before, in San Jose, his motorcade had been overrun by nine hundred demonstrators who turned out with placards that read "Nixon = Fascist" and "Nixon—Get Us Out Now." In what United Press International called "the most violent protest he has faced since taking office," Nixon felt an egg graze his cheek and had to duck into his limousine to escape rocks and bottles. The caravan sped away to the chant, "One, two, three, four, we don't want your war."

Emerging from his plane at the Hughes Air Terminal in a charcoal-gray suit, Nixon tried to draw a distinction between the young people he saw before him and the protesters from the evening before.

"Violence makes news in the press, but I think young America is getting a bad rap from these violent, radical few," he said. "Those who carry a peace sign in one hand and carry a bomb or a brick in the other are the top hypocrites of our time. The great silent majority should stand up and be counted in the polling booths throughout this great land."

Still, the deck was stacked against Nevada's Republicans. Without their popular governor, Paul Laxalt, on the ballot to counteract the Democrats' edge in voter registration, they lost every major contest on Election Day. They surrendered the governor's mansion, several U.S. House districts, seats in both chambers of the state legislature, and the office of the lieutenant governor, which went to a thirty-year-old assemblyman and former amateur boxer named Harry Reid.

The midterm election of 1970 might have started out as a sleepy affair, but it produced two forces that would be powerful staples of American politics for the next half century: Reid and the War on Drugs. It also had a profound effect on Sonny Liston. Because when it came to drawing the attention of federal law enforcement, Sonny was becoming a junkie at exactly the wrong time.

11.

——

LOVE, AMERICAN STYLE

FROM "Criswell Predicts,"
Fabulous Las Vegas, November 1970

Here is a hush hush hush prediction! Mysterious cracks in the floor of the ocean are appearing, not only on the Pacific Coast but also on the Atlantic Coast! Those cracks are up to 50 feet wide and ten miles long! Our Scientists are puzzled and if our Scientists are puzzled, we should be terrified!

With the trucker movie *Moonfire* set for release in 1971, Sonny's acting career was beginning to take off. Maybe he wasn't ready for *The Godfather*, which was the hottest property in Hollywood. As the *Sun*'s entertainment writer Ralph Pearl reported, "Every big star from Edward G. Robinson to Anthony Quinn, Rod Steiger, Ernie Borgnine and John Marley . . . down to San Francisco mouthpiece Melvin Belli [is] begging for the part. Even Danny Thomas wants a crack at that role." But there was a place for Sonny's type of tough guy in the string of blaxploitation movies that were about to swamp America. Gordon Parks's *Shaft* would debut in 1971, setting off a genre race with franchise pictures like *Super Fly*, *Foxy Brown*, and *Blacula*. Two years later, the studios wouldn't be able to pump out sequels fast enough, explaining the celluloid gifts that were *Shaft in Africa*, *Scream Blacula Scream*, and *Super Fly T.N.T.*

Hollywood was crashing between two decades. At the Academy Awards back in April, sixty-two-year-old John Wayne received his first Oscar for portraying an aging marshal in *True Grit*. But the award for best film went to the far grittier *Midnight Cowboy*, an X-rated story of a male hooker braving the streets of New York. Television was in flux, too. In a couple of months *All in the Family* would debut on CBS. For the moment the network's Friday-night lineup offered a television show adapted from the medical movie *The Interns*, as well as a new star vehicle for Andy Griffith and a movie of the week. NBC was slightly more adventurous. It paired an old-fashioned western, *The High Chaparral*, with a big-budget police serial, *The Name of the Game*, and a back-lot Hollywood drama called *Bracken's World*. ABC, meanwhile, went for family comedies:

The Brady Bunch at 7:30 p.m., followed by *Nanny and the Professor*, *The Partridge Family*, and the fifth season of *That Girl*. At 9:30 it slipped in the anthology *Love, American Style*.

Compared with the other shows, *Love* was risqué. Its sly look at sex in 1970 pushed boundaries for its time, even though it used well-known actors from the fifties and early sixties. When executive producer Arnold Margolin got a script for an episode called "Love and the Champ," he thought it was a no-brainer to reach out to Sonny. "I figured it was a one-scene role," Margolin would recall. "We could contain the damage if it didn't work out." For Sonny, the gig was a no-brainer, too. It would give him an excuse to go to L.A., pocket an easy thousand bucks, and party.

When it came time for his 6:00 a.m. camera call on the Paramount lot, Sonny showed up looking like he hadn't slept in days. Margolin welcomed his guest star warmly. But Sonny wasn't in the mood to be congenial. In fact, he snarled when Margolin told him that the script he'd been sent had undergone a few changes. It's likely that Sonny was too embarrassed to say he couldn't read the changes. Instead he said simply, "I do the lines I learned."

"It was the only time I ever felt threatened by an actor," Margolin would say. "I figured it wasn't worth getting killed for an eight-minute segment."

The filming took place in the summer, with the airdate scheduled for Thanksgiving. "The timing was perfect," Margolin added. "It was a turkey."

A s the Listons prepared to celebrate Thanksgiving at home, Sonny got into his Caddy for a quick trip into town. There's no telling where he was going. To see his mistress? To make a quick trip to the Westside to score? To place a bet at the International? Maybe it was all three. Or maybe Geraldine had just run out of cooking broth and needed him to go to the store. It didn't matter.

As he'd done a thousand times before, Sonny pulled out of their development and pulled onto East Desert Inn Road, heading west toward the Strip. After a mile and a quarter, he reached Cayuga Parkway and started to make a left when the driver of a Mercury came speeding down the parkway in the opposite direction. The Mercury was going so fast that Sonny had no time to react to an impact that was swift and intense. His Eldorado went screeching into a telephone pole, hitting with such force that it nearly folded in half. Sonny's chest went into the steering wheel, literally bending it as his head plowed into the windshield.

By the time paramedics arrived at the scene, Sonny had staggered out of the car, his face covered in blood from the glass shards embedded in it. An ambulance took him to Sunrise Hospital, where plastic surgeons worked laboriously to pull out each piece of glass, one at a time. It was excruciating work, and Sonny, who was still in mild shock, suffered it quietly. According to Lem Banker, who rushed to the hospital, the only thing that bothered him was the shot of anesthesia that he got. After all he'd been through, he still hated needles that much.

Sonny was sent home that night for what was a less than relaxing Thanksgiving. And the next evening, while he was still recovering, he settled in with a few friends to see himself on *Love, American Style*.

If he was inclined to be amused at the way he looked in a situation comedy, he had a hard time doing it out loud. With twenty stitches in his head and a citation beside him for failing to yield the right of way, it hurt to laugh. And the next day, Saturday, November 28, he still wasn't right. He felt pains in his chest, the kind that a man his age shouldn't be feeling. Sonny told Geraldine, who loaded him up in her green Caddy and took him to Southern Nevada Memorial Hospital.

That month, *The Ring* magazine ranked him fourth in the heavyweight division, which was four spots higher than he'd been just a few months earlier. But there was something nagging about this injury, something that made him feel mortal. Geraldine was pushing for him to retire, as was his friend Davey Pearl, and he was beginning to think they were right. Given the way his blood pressure had been going up, it probably wasn't a bad idea for him to chill out for a few days and enjoy some heavy medication.

On Wednesday, December 2, while he was still under sedation, Sonny opened the *Las Vegas Sun* to see a story on the third page about his accident: "Former Boxing Champ Liston Hospitalized Here After Auto Wreck." "I don't think it's going to keep me from fighting," he told the paper, trying to sound optimistic. "But you can't always tell about these things. I feel as well as I expected to."

His story, however, was overshadowed by this banner headline on the front page:

HOWARD HUGHES VANISHES!
MYSTERY BAFFLES CLOSE ASSOCIATES

By Hank Greenspun

SUN PUBLISHER (COPYRIGHT LAS VEGAS SUN 1970)

Howard Hughes, often called the phantom financier since he established permanent residence in Las Vegas in 1966, is involved in a disappearance from Nevada under circumstances even more mysterious than his secrecy-shrouded arrival.

The billionaire industrialist arrived in Las Vegas on Thanksgiving eve and the Sun learned yesterday he vanished from his Desert Inn residence on the exact date four years later.

Las Vegans have long been intrigued by the story that Hughes came to Las Vegas on a special train from which he alighted at a remote desert siding and was whisked to his specially prepared quarters at the Desert Inn.

That story pales in comparison with the facts of his departure. . . .

———

Howard Hughes first arrived in Las Vegas on November 23, 1966, in a pair of private Pullman railcars with their curtains drawn. As his biographers Donald Barlett and James Steele would recount, the journey "symbolized a complete break with [his] past." The billionaire was looking to leave Hollywood, where he'd lived since he started making pictures in 1925, and he rented the top two floors of the Desert Inn for what was initially planned as a ten-day vacation. He saw so much building potential along the Strip, however, that he wound up buying the hotel, putting down the then-considerable sum of $6.2 million.

Hughes wasted no time throwing his influence around. He seduced leading politicians with promises to move his aerospace interests into Nevada and offered to finance a medical school on the University of Nevada's campus that had been imperiled by budget cuts. Even though he hadn't been seen in public for nearly five years and neglected to supply a mandatory photo of himself, the news that Nevada's newest billionaire was so civic-minded allowed his gaming application to sail through.

At least initially, the city's district attorney, George Franklin, saw Hughes as a long-awaited counterweight to the mob. "The best way to improve the image of gambling in Nevada is by licensing an industrialist of his stature," he said upon Hughes's arrival. But a few years later Franklin was regretting his enthusiasm. Hughes's tangle of shell companies was drawing questions from U.S. stock regulators. At a Lions Club dinner, Franklin alluded to Hughes's holdings by telling his audience, "We have received more bad publicity with [his] corporations than we did when we had . . . the Purple Gang and the Cleveland mob."

But, unlike Bugsy Siegel and the others who built Las Vegas, Hughes had a vision that was iterative. Where the old-timers brought Hollywood glamour, Hughes wanted a more updated, urban version of discretion and class. "I like to think of Las Vegas in terms of a well-dressed man in a dinner jacket and a furred female getting out of an expensive car," he wrote. "I think that is what the people expect here—to rub shoulders with V.I.P.'s and stars."

While Hughes kept himself holed up in his penthouse at the Desert Inn with the windows blacked out, feverishly writing longhand memos at all hours of the night, he relied on an ex–FBI agent, Robert Maheu, to help him juggle his interests.

Maheu rose quickly in Hughes's orbit. With nearly complete discretion to manage the billionaire's sprawling $300 million Nevada empire, he moved his family into a half-million-dollar mansion in Paradise Palms and threw his boss's influence around with remarkable aplomb. He held opulent society parties at his home, attended ribbon cuttings, and offered what purported to be Hughes's opinions when reporters phoned for comments on Nevada's affairs.

Even though he never actually met Hughes in person, getting all his instructions by wire or over the phone, Maheu also managed to keep the billionaire from making some headstrong mistakes, such as when Hughes became so paranoid about radiation leakage from the underground nuclear tests in the desert that he wanted to offer Richard Nixon a million-dollar bribe to end them.

The problem for Maheu was that his power rested solely on his relationship with Hughes, and that left him vulnerable to a whisper campaign from the executives who had been left behind at Hughes headquarters at 7000 Romaine Street in Los Angeles. The head of that faction was a sober, well-schooled executive named Frank William "Bill" Gay.

Like the others in his orbit, Gay resented Maheu's quick ascent in Hughes's chain of command and the fact that he was secretly using the profits they created in California to mask his huge deficits in Nevada. Hughes's Las Vegas operation had lost $3.8 million in 1968 and $8.4 million in 1969, and was on a pace to lose a staggering $14 million in 1970.

Midway through 1970, Gay confronted Hughes about the deficits. Several sudden shocks, including a $180 million judgment in a decade-old case involving Trans World Airlines, had left him with barely $20 million in working funds for the year. All of a sudden Maheu's spiraling debt was no joke.

Hughes began to listen to the criticisms that he'd previously ignored and even to intimations that Maheu had stolen hundreds of thousands of dollars to finance his lofty lifestyle. In a sudden burst of suspicion, Hughes called for an audit of his entire Las Vegas operation while green-lighting a transfer of power to Gay.

On Thanksgiving Eve, a phalanx of limousines with California license plates surrounded the Desert Inn and a small army of men emerged to take Hughes out of the ninth-floor complex he'd occupied in seclusion for four years. The story splashed across the front page of the *Sun* reflected Maheu's estrangement:

"Even those closest to [Hughes] in Nevada operations were left in total bewilderment. . . . The absence of an explanation creates disturbing and disquieting conjectures." Grasping at straws, Maheu admitted that he "could shed no light on the strange development" and suggested that Gay's Romaine Group may have abducted Hughes.

The disappearance was the only thing anyone in Las Vegas could talk about for days. A public relations firm tried to quell the furor by insisting that Hughes was just on a business trip, but that half-truth didn't go far. The reality was that a civil war had broken out.

While Sonny still lay hospitalized, Gay swept into Las Vegas to set up his own command center on the top floor of the Sands. Unleashing an army of auditors on Hughes's casinos, he seized the money and chips in the cashiers' cages and sent Maheu a message telling him that he had until sunset to resign.

Gay, however, underestimated the small-town politics of Las Vegas. Using his contacts at the *Sun*, Maheu issued a statement warning that a rogue group of corporate pirates had initiated "an authorized takeover of the operations of Mr. Howard Hughes' properties." He also obtained a federal order to restrain Gay from looting the casinos. The *Sun* played along by noting it was the anniversary of Pearl Harbor and referring to Gay's group as an "invading faction." When Gay's lawyer suggested that they should sell Hughes's casinos if this was the way they were going to be treated, it led to another spasm of local suspicion about newcomers' intentions.

The politicians who relied on Maheu's generosity were in a

quandary about what to do. The governor, Paul Laxalt, suggested that Hughes return to Las Vegas to make his feelings known. But Hughes, who was hiding in the Bahamas, was in no condition to return. Recovering from a bout of pneumonia, he was down to ninety-five pounds and could not stand on his own. Instead, he told Gay to invite Laxalt to the Sands for an extraordinary 1:30 a.m. phone call in which the billionaire assured him that he'd personally approved Maheu's ouster.

Laxalt left the Sands convinced that Hughes was both coherent and in command, and in one of his last acts as governor he phoned Maheu to say it would be in everyone's interests if he gave up.

But Maheu and his loyalists remained undeterred. A Las Vegas attorney with close ties to the ex–FBI agent heightened the drama by telling a packed press conference that someone who was masquerading as Hughes had been on the phone with Laxalt. "If I was convinced these were the wishes of Mr. Hughes, I would leave forthwith," said the attorney, Tom Bell, casting a knowing glance around the room. He also warned the packed room of reporters that Hughes was in grave danger because his abductors had left "vital climate control devices necessary to insure his proper breathing" at the Desert Inn.

With both sides locked in a high-stakes standoff, Gay finally went to federal court to get his own restraining order, setting the stage for a showdown over the future of Hughes's fortune the likes of which Las Vegas had never seen, and which completely overshadowed the foundering fortunes of a hospitalized heavyweight.

A cross the country, in New York on December 7, fight fans were hoping to see a brawl of at least equal caliber. As a sellout crowd streamed into Madison Square Garden to see Muhammad Ali face Oscar Bonavena, a photographer for *Life* magazine captured men sporting walking sticks, clad in capes, and wearing pinstriped suits paired with polar-bear-white fur hats.

Although Ali didn't look particularly sharp against Jerry Quarry in Atlanta, he appeared to have providence on his side this time around. After the weigh-in at the Garden, a basketball player who was practicing for a game that night tossed Ali a ball at half court. The promoter, Harry Markson, later recalled watching Ali heave the ball, "and I'll be damned if it didn't go in, *swish*. Everyone just stared in awe but that was the kind of luck I figured followed Ali."

Ali figured he was lucky, too. The day of the fight, he stayed up until 6:00 a.m. talking with friends about the potential of his showdown with Joe Frazier, all the while seeming to look past Bonavena. It's understandable why Ali was so focused on the future. An appeals court had just reaffirmed his draft-dodging conviction, meaning he had only a few months of freedom unless the U.S. Supreme Court did the improbable and stepped in to save him.

In boxing terms, he was in the fifteenth round of his legal case and needed a knockout to win.

Bonavena, however, wasn't a fighter who deserved to be overlooked. His Hall of Fame trainer, Gil Clancy, had spent a lot of time watching Ali and developed a shrewd strategy: Bonavena would let himself get worked into the corners to cut down on the angles that Ali liked to use to use and then strike. "When he punches, he has to be attached to his arm," Clancy told him. "So if he hits you or misses the punch, either way, he's at the other end of that arm."

When the bell clanged at the Garden just before 11:00 p.m., Bonavena leapt from his corner in a crouching stance to start slinging punches right away. For all the hours Ali had spent sparring, he never anticipated a tough fight, and now he was getting a rude awakening. "Every day in the gym he'd talk Frazier," Angelo Dundee told the writer Michael Arkush. "I finally had to show him Bonavena's picture and tell him, this is who you are fighting." The Garden mischievously paired Howard Cosell at ringside with Joe Frazier's manager, Yank Durham, and Durham couldn't help needling his fighter's next opponent. "Clay definitely don't have what he had before," he said. "I can see that."

Through the early rounds, Ali fought flat-footed and absorbed some powerful punches. "Strange thing to see. You've not seen Ali like this before," a mystified Cosell said at the end of the fourth, and by the seventh, when Bonavena was gaining strength: "This is not the Ali style at all, at least as how it *used* to exist."

Traces of the old Ali finally began to emerge midway through the ninth round when a Bonavena punch to his head awakened him and he responded with a flurry of jabs, uppercuts, and crosses. With a minute left in the round, Ali opened a cut over

Bonavena's eye. But the men were so exhausted by the exchange that they spent the rest of the fight swinging at air. "There's no doubt in my mind he's a worried fighter," Durham said of Ali in the tenth, and after the eleventh: "I don't know if he'll even be able to continue this fight."

By the beginning of the fifteenth round, fans were booing Ali, although he was ahead on points. Durham, sensing that his earlier criticisms might have been a bit overheated, hedged by telling Cosell, "Howard, I still have Ali ahead on points but if Bonavena can win this round it will be a very tough fight to judge." Cosell, ever the reporter, jumped in with a question: "Now, all right. If Ali should win this round by a decision, Yancey, will his performance tonight affect a potential fight against your man, Frazier?"

At that point fans in Timbuktu could smell Durham smelling the money. "No, Howard. I think this is a fight the public want to see, and I'm glad to see, if he wins this fight, it goes to fifteen rounds. I think it put him in good condition."

As the final round began, Ali snapped his head back to avoid one of Bonavena's wildest punches, but Cosell was skeptical. "You saw Oscar at his wildest there, missing, falling off balance, but there was no Ali to take advantage of it," he complained. "There was no speed left. There was no movement left."

But then, suddenly, there was.

With a minute and thirty seconds left to the fight, Bonavena let his guard down long enough for Ali to take the express train home. In close quarters, he found a path to Bonavena's head and gave him a thunderous straight-ahead jab. Before the crowd could process what had happened, Bonavena staggered like someone who'd been shot unknowingly from a distance and fallen. "Oh, that left!" Cosell shouted. "It came from nowhere." Bonavena staggered to his feet but two more punches ended it.

In the corner, amid the pandemonium, Ali kept his eye on the prize he was fighting for. "The layoff bothered me," he told Cosell. "I missed a lot of punches. But I'm glad it was the war it was. . . . Now we have the chance to see who the real champion of the world is."

Shortly after the Bonavena fight, two executives of Madison Square Garden took a train to Philadelphia to make Frazier the long-awaited offer to face Ali.

Frazier had gotten his start in 1965 with the backing of a syndicate that bought eighty shares in him for $250 apiece. Since then, those shares had split five times, yielding a paper value of $14,400 each. "If Frazier were to retire tomorrow, he'd get $218,000 in cold cash," one of the group's directors told *The Ring* magazine. Half of that was invested for Frazier and the other half was distributed as a weekly salary of $400. In addition, a trust fund had been set up for his four kids.

Frazier had been anticipating the fight with Ali for some time. In late 1969, the two ran into each other in Philadelphia's Fairmount Park, where Frazier did his daily four-mile run. Ali began kicking up dust and shadowboxing and soon a crowd gathered, urging the men on. As Frazier would later recall, "Clay being Clay, he put up his hands and started jiving. He liked to do that with guys who were future opponents. He wanted to measure them to see if he could hit them." Frazier pushed his hands away, but instead of backing off, Ali flicked a left and shouted, "Let's get it on right here."

Frazier liked Ali and was shrewd enough to understand his antics. (This was, after all, the same twenty-six-year-old fighter who played with his band, the Knockouts, in the lounge of Caesars; show business wasn't a foreign concept.) So he went along with the gag and suggested that they meet at a local gym run by the Police Athletic League. What he didn't count on was that Ali would arrive in his trunks with hundreds of spectators and swamp the tiny gym. The cops who showed up weren't amused and told the men to take their rumble back to Fairmont Park.

A few years earlier, all Ali had to do was show up on the tarmac at Miami's airport and call Liston "an ugly bear" to get headlines. But the bar for him was higher now. What he said carried weight. And as he jumped into his red convertible and drove off, he yelled at Frazier, "He wants to prove he's the champ. Let him prove it here in the ghetto, where the colored folks can see it."

By the time Frazier's manager, Yank Durham, got wind of what was going on, he put an end to the stunt. But instead of deciding that he'd milked their chance encounter for all he could, Ali continued his crude attacks on Frazier. In his interview with *The Black Scholar*, he singled out Frazier for dating a white woman and summed up his contributions to boxing by saying, "Now the white man's got the heavyweight champion."

The remark blindsided Frazier. The last thing he expected was for Ali to come into his city acting what he called all "high-hat on me." And he really didn't like Ali "talking about me as if I was some head-scratching dumb nigger." In his autobiography, Frazier would write, "[It was] cruel and unworthy. And in its way, sadistic, like pulling the wings off a dying insect. . . . Clay knew . . . the struggle a black man had, growing up in Beaufort, South Carolina. [He] knew that in saying what he did, he was playing me cheap and leaving Joe Frazier, and his children, open to ridicule—worse, he was encouraging it."

It's possible that Ali was using Frazier to burnish his black credentials in case he needed them in prison. Or maybe he figured that if he couldn't fight Frazier, he'd tarnish the reigning champion's title in any way that he could. After Frazier beat Ellis at Madison Square Garden the next January, he returned to his hotel room dead tired. When the phone rang, he picked it up to hear Ali on the other end. As he later said to reporters:

"I told him I don't want no foolishness. I'm tired of the [Muslim] changes he been going through and the poem thing, and I don't want being shoved or slapped by him on the street no more. I'm not saying Cassius has the mind of a child, but that sort of stuff's for kids trying to pick a fight. I want him to grow up and maybe someday we'll be able to settle it. I don't feel Clay or anyone else can whup me."

Maybe that was true. But Ali, the committed pacifist, was clearly prepared to use the politics of personal destruction to get an edge for a fight that hadn't even been arranged yet.

And sadly, it worked. The Madison Square Garden executives arrived in Philadelphia with an offer that dwarfed anything Frazier had anticipated. They were ready to guarantee him $1.25

million to fight Ali in New York. As Arkush noted in *The Fight of the Century*, Frazier tried jotting the figure down but stumbled because he had no idea where to put the commas.

The Garden executives assumed they had an inside track, because Frazier had fought there seven times, most recently in February, when he unified the heavyweight title by beating Jimmy Ellis. What they didn't see coming—what no one did— was the out-of-left-field interest of a talent agent best known for representing the likes of Elton John, Elizabeth Taylor, and Glen Campbell.

Jerry Perenchio didn't have any clients in boxing but he loved the pageantry that surrounded the Ali–Quarry fight when he saw it via closed circuit in Los Angeles and decided right then that he wanted to produce Ali's fight with Frazier. When he started reaching out to his very rich Hollywood clients, however, he was surprised to discover that they didn't share his enthusiasm for spending $5 million to secure the rights. He'd exhausted most of his Rolodex before he finally called one of the most prominent owners in sports to ask for a lunch.

With teams in the NFL (Washington Redskins), the NHL (Los Angeles Kings), and the NBA (Los Angeles Lakers), Jack Kent Cooke understood big events. He also hosted fights at his Forum in Inglewood. And his eyes lit up in his Los Angeles office when Perenchio described his vision for a spectacular that would transcend boxing. As he'd later say, "[Perenchio] was the greatest salesman I ever knew. He epitomized a positive attitude."

The beauty of what they worked out was that neither actually put up a cent. Cooke provided a $4.5 million letter of credit against the eventual proceeds, and in order to keep the fight in New York—not in the Houston Astrodome, which was also lobbying heavily for it—the Madison Square Garden executives threw in the remaining $500,000. "Once Jerry put $2.5 million out there for each fighter, it was case closed," promoter Bob Arum would recall. "That blew everyone's mind. No fighter had ever made anything like that in the history of boxing. Not Jack Dempsey, not Gene Tunney, not Louis."

Sonny was following those negotiations closely. And according to a never-before-reported incident, he was already counting the cash he was going to get from his cut.

T he details of the deal that Sonny may have struck with the Nation of Islam on the eve of Sonny's rematch with Ali in 1965 have never been fleshed out. And they may end up being unknowable. But according to a former Nevada state assemblyman, Sonny was under the clear impression that he was entitled to a cut of Ali's $2.5 million guarantee.

One afternoon in December 1970, after he got out of the hospital, he was at Friendly Liquor Store, drinking vodka and playing rummy with his sidekicks, when they started asking him about the reports they'd read that Frazier was close to coming to terms with Ali. Listening in was a twenty-seven-year-old electrician named Gene Collins. Years later, after he became a Nevada state assemblyman and a two-term president of the Las Vegas

NAACP, Collins would sit in the lounge at Jerry's Nugget Casino, not far from where Friendly's stood, and recall how Sonny got more and more animated as they talked about the size of Ali's paycheck.

"This is the first time I've ever mentioned this because I don't usually talk about stuff like that," Collins told me. "But Sonny was shooting his mouth off that he had a portion of Ali's contract. I thought it was awful strange that he'd be saying something like that. It was definitely out of place, if you ask me. Everybody was kind of stunned. He was drinking. But to come out and say that . . ."

Collins wasn't the only one who heard Sonny make the claim. His friend Clyde "Rabbit" Watkins said the same thing when I met him in his home. "We was at the Cove Hotel and he told me, 'I'm gonna get some money as long as Ali is fighting.' How much, I don't know. But he said he'd have money for the rest of his life."

The twin recollections—offered separately and without prompting—suggest that Sonny was counting on Ali to support him now that his fighting career was done. Whether a deal really existed wasn't necessarily the point. Sonny *believed* a deal existed.

The disclosures also explain why some very powerful people might have started to worry that Sonny was talking too much about the money he was going to get from Ali . . . too much for his—and their—own good.

12.

—————

STUNG

John Sutton hit Las Vegas just as the Christmas season of 1970 was beginning. Wayne Newton was at the Frontier. The Smothers Brothers were at Caesars. The Wonderful World of Burlesque was kicking it up at the Silver Slipper. This was Las Vegas at its best, manufacturing a snowy wonderland of tinsel and showgirls out of once worthless desert real estate.

After his last trip, in which his boss's informant had embarrassingly made him, Sutton decided to tone things down. He ditched the flashy Buick Electra 225 with the horn that blared "La Cucaracha" for a four-door Cadillac Eldorado (albeit still in baby blue) and made his way to the Bureau of Narcotics and Dangerous Drugs to meet the informant who'd been supplying them information about Sonny. To be inconspicuous, he used the unmarked door in back that was usually reserved for secret witnesses.

Sonny's accident had been all over the news. But after his discharge from Southern Nevada Memorial Hospital on December 8, he didn't waste any time picking up where he left off. He went to his Cadillac dealership to pick up a new 1971 Fleetwood and drove straight to the International, where he was aggressively hustling fifty- and hundred-dollar bags of coke.

Sutton was eager to land Liston. And not just for the drugs he would take off the street. What he knew about the fight game alone—about Ali and Louis and half the promoters in the sport—could make an agent's career. If Sutton did his job right, Sonny would be testifying in front of grand juries for the rest of his life.

He went over his options with Robinson, the station chief. They could apply for a wiretap to listen in on his calls, but that would take time; worse, in the leaky world of Las Vegas law enforcement, there was an above-average risk that Sonny would find out that the feds were onto him. They could also set up surveillance, but chances were the local cops would get wind of that, too. The strategy that Sutton liked best was more discreet, and known in the trade as "one, two, three and a cloud of dust."

In the first step, a source introduced you to the target to establish your false identity. If it worked, it led to a second meeting without the source where you could make a small buy on your own. The third meeting was the crucial one. It was where you made a larger buy, cementing the relationship and setting up a fourth buy, which was so much larger that the target had to bring in his supplier, and maybe even the supplier above him. That was when you swept in and left them all busted in a cloud of dust.

Sutton told his informant that they'd hit the International the next afternoon. In the meantime he checked back into the Villa Roma, got himself a meal, and played an hour of quarter slots before hitting the sack. When he awoke, he went to the gym, got a big lunch, and was ready to go when his sidekick showed up at his hotel. Per his usual routine, Sutton frisked his partner to make sure he wasn't holding a gun or drugs—he wasn't—and checked his wallet to see how much cash he had. He counted about twenty bucks and handed back the money, making a mental note to check the wallet again when they were all done so he could confirm the guy wasn't double-dealing on the side. Then he looked at his own billfold. He'd signed out a thousand dollars from the BNDD's safe, mostly fifties with a few hundreds. Each bill was marked for identification.

Next, the agent went over their cover story. He wanted to be introduced as the snitch's gangster cousin from Salt Lake City who was looking for a quick score. Making sure that he dressed the part, he wore a long leather coat with cow-skin lapels and a leather hat. Once he was satisfied they had their story straight, he opened the door of his Eldorado and they drove off.

Even in midweek, the International was impressive. Its thirty-thousand-square-foot gaming hall was packed with tourists, and plenty more were on the spectacular eight-and-a-half-acre rooftop playground that was just a floor up. The two men blended into the crowd, making their way past the slot machines and the blackjack tables to the keno area, where they grabbed a pair of seats in the lounge.

Keno, in which a player picks numbers with the hope of matching the digits on Ping-Pong balls that are fed from a fishbowl by a blower, can be a tedious game, and Sutton settled in to play a few hands, which turned into a few more, which all of a sudden turned into five hours' worth—enough for him to drink three Tom Collinses and eat more than he had intended. Along the way, he asked a few waitresses if they'd seen Sonny and was assured that he was usually there. By eight in the evening, when there was no sight of him, the snitch suggested, "We could see if he's home."

Sutton considered this. His whole plan relied on the introduction. He didn't want to screw that up. And since it was already past dinnertime, Sonny might be suspicious if a stranger suddenly showed up. Even if he wasn't, approaching him like that at home seemed like an unnecessary risk. Sutton drove to Ottawa Drive just to get a feel for the place—quiet, winding streets, not too many people peering out their windows; all in all, a good spot to deal drugs—but then he called it a night.

The next day he met his informant at his motel, repeated his safety checks, and drove to the International for a second try. This time, to his relief, he spotted the hulking figure of his target right away in the keno lounge. The agent kept his distance as Sonny disappeared behind the cashier's cage, but a half hour passed, and then another, and when he didn't return, Sutton decided to stir things up. He went to the house phone and told the operator, "I'd like to page Charles Liston."

Sonny was snorting cocaine on the can when the message crackled through the public address system: *"Charles Liston. Please meet your friends in the keno area."*

The page sent a shooting pain through his head. The only ones who called him Charles anymore were Geraldine, the fans who read about him in the papers, and the cops. His money was on the cops. But the locals knew where to find him, and they always called him Sonny.

Charles. He closed his eyes and tried to think straight. It had to be the feds. But which ones? It was in all the papers that the FBI was crawling over every square inch of Caesars Palace. After spending months investigating its top layer of management for taking sports bets over the phone in violation of the federal Wire Act, agents swept down on the resort at nine in the morning and went straight to the office of its executive vice president, Sandy Waterman, the same casino boss who'd belted Frank Sinatra. While agents in twenty-five other cities were arresting two dozen of the biggest sports bettors in the country, the agents cuffed Waterman and four other executives, including Sonny's neighbor on Ottawa Drive, Frank Masterana. In Washington, U.S. attorney general John Mitchell described the Caesars executives as "the illegal underwriters for the top bookmakers in the nation."

Ash Resnick wasn't caught up in the raid. But who knew who was ratting on whom?

"Charles Liston. Your friends are waiting for you at the keno area."

Sonny wasn't about to wait to find out. He finished his business, pulled up his trousers, washed his hands, and made his way into the keno room. He scanned the cashier's desk and the gaming tables beyond it and triangulated a shortcut to the exit. Knowing he'd stand out, he swept past the slots and weaved his way through the craps tables until he reached the revolving door. Not bothering to look behind him, he placed a bill in the hand of the valet for his Caddy and drove off.

When he assured himself that he wasn't being followed, he let out a deep breath.

Charles Liston. Shit.

Sutton was waiting in the lounge when he saw Sonny race out of the bathroom behind the cashier's cage. He tried following Sonny as he made a beeline for the door, but by the time he got to his car, Sonny was already in his Cadillac, speeding away. Instead of trailing him back to his house, Sutton decided to be patient and give the International one last try the next day.*

On Sunday, December 13, he took up his position in the keno lounge, where the waitresses had conveniently come to think of him as a regular, and started playing the numbers. Whatever had spooked Liston must still be spooking him, Sutton thought, because he was a no-show. This time Sutton decided to play his last card. "Come on, we're getting out of here,"

---

*The dates are according to Sutton's review of his itinerary.

he told his informant, and the two made the ten-minute drive to Ottawa Drive.

He could see from the twin Cadillacs parked in front of the two-car garage that someone was home. Sutton parked in front of the lemon tree in the yard while his informant got out and walked up the long white steps to the art deco façade and rang the doorbell. It was a cool December afternoon, a wintry 56 degrees, and Sutton was impressed to see Sonny answer in charcoal pants and a tight-fitting T-shirt. Sutton was a big man but Sonny was bigger.

The agent couldn't hear what the men were saying, but he saw Sonny's pencil mustache twitch and worried that something might be going wrong. His informant kept talking and made enough headway that after a minute he waved Sutton over. More than forty years later, Sutton would still recall the way Sonny stuck out his hand when the informant introduced him as his cousin John from Salt Lake. In all his years dealing with tough guys, he'd never seen a hand so big. When Sutton shook it, it swallowed his own.

Geraldine was cooking in the kitchen and Sonny made no move to introduce the men when he escorted them through the living room and into his den. As they all sat down, Sutton tried to break the ice by mentioning that he'd been following Sonny's career since the Patterson days. He was relieved when Sonny broke out into a grin. "Yeah, man, you can't believe how much white pussy I used to get," he replied, dropping his voice so Geraldine wouldn't hear him. "White pussy everywhere." He was boastful, but also relaxed and friendly, and he crinkled his nose when the informant asked him whether he had any coke for sale.

No, he said apologetically. He'd done it all the day before. "I was in the bathroom doing lines," Sonny explained. "I don't know how long it was, but it was a long time. And while I was in there somebody paged me calling me Charles. Ain't no motherfucker in the world but the police calls me Charles. I was so high, I even forgot that was my name. And the motherfucker paged me several times. A buddy of mine who works in the hotel told me the place was crawlin' with the police. I thanked him but I don't give a fuck."

Sutton cursed himself for another rookie mistake. *Charles.* How could he be so stupid? Well, at least now he knew why Sonny had left the International looking spooked.

The informant, still working, asked Sonny if he had something small lying around the house. "You know, just a little stamp for your man?"

"Shit, if I do it ain't a lot," Sonny said.

He told the men to wait while he went to his bedroom to look. It was tempting in that moment—left alone with the man's accomplishments in his room, in his house—for Sutton to see something tragic in Liston. After all, boxing existed to cheat its brightest stars. Sonny belonged to the generation where money disappeared down rat holes that were dug by rats. Maybe with just a little more support, a little more education, he might have . . .

Sutton stared at the photo of Sonny shaking hands with President Lyndon Johnson. No, best not to go down that road. The guy had had plenty of opportunities. Keep it simple. He was just another bad guy dealing drugs and ruining neighborhoods.

A few minutes later Sonny returned with a look of genuine disappointment. "I thought I had some on my night table but Geraldine musta cleaned it," he said. "Probably thought it was headache powder or something. She don't know nothin' 'bout this stuff."

Sutton tried to gauge if something had spooked Sonny. Did he suddenly get suspicious? Did he put two and two together and see that the answer to who had paged him at the International was staring him right in the face?

If so, he didn't seem overly concerned. He went on about his accident and how the medication he was given in the hospital, morphine or maybe Dilaudid, left him so high he didn't want to leave. Sutton waited until Sonny stopped talking before redirecting the conversation. Using the old police trick of distracting a source by getting him to look into the future, he asked: "So, when you gonna get some more?"

Sonny had a contact in Los Angeles who hooked him up on a regular basis, usually with a pound of cocaine at a time. But because of his accident he hadn't been able to make his regular trip. He was, however, going in a few days. "I'm staying in Henderson and I really don't wanna drive all the way to L.A.," Sutton said. "I was really hoping to set up a pound connection here in Las Vegas."

Sonny nodded. The last time he made the trip, he said, a cop flagged him while he was driving with two condoms full of coke under the front seat. He had to cut them and throw them out the window before pulling over to the side. Fortunately, the highway patrol officer let him go with a warning. "All the big white folk here like me," he said, implying that he understood why Sutton, without the same celebrity, would have qualms about driving between states with a pound of cocaine. "How about I score a pound for you when I go?" he asked.

Cousin John smiled and said he appreciated it. Then they rose to shake on the deal. Step one was done. On to steps two and three and the cloud of dust.

At about 7:30 p.m. on December 16, 1970, a California Highway Patrol officer was sitting in his cruiser on the San Bernardino Freeway when he noticed a Cadillac swerving in and out of the eastbound lanes. Flipping on his flashing lights, he pulled behind the Caddy and brought it to a stop on the side of the road. He must not have known who Sonny was, because after he asked for his license, he asked, "What do you do, sir?"

It was then, according to an account in the *Los Angeles Sentinel*, that Sonny provided the answer "I'm a boxer. *Unemployed.*"

What a thing to say to a cop! He didn't say that he was a celebrity, or a businessman, or even an actor, which is what everyone said in L.A. He said he was unemployed. It was a depressing statement, the kind that someone who'd been drinking hard and wallowing in self-pity would make. In fact, the cop described him as being "moody." That evening he was brought to the Los Angeles PD's central booking unit and charged with drunken driving. He paid $308 in cash to get out.

Why was he moody? Why wouldn't he be? Ever since the accident, he hadn't felt quite right. Not frail, exactly, but not the same intimidating force that he had been. In a weirdly prescient metaphor, Sonny once told *The Washington Post*: "Fighters are just like cars. You get in a car and put your foot on the pedal down to the floorboard and that car's not gonna last long. If the car has just one owner and that owner takes it easy, then that car's gonna last a long time."

The foot was about as far down on that floorboard as it could go. Sonny had been arrested and hospitalized twice in the space of a month and was probably in California to get the cocaine he'd promised Sutton that he'd bring back. *Moody?* Damn right he was moody. Here he was, hustling fifty-dollar bags of coke to support himself, and every time he heard another dollar figure thrown around about the Ali–Frazier fight, he got moodier.

Even Geraldine, who managed Sonny better than anybody, was at her wit's end with his mood swings. Shortly before Christmas, one of his oldest friends, Lowell Powell, a retired St. Louis policeman who'd worked as a bodyguard for Sonny over the years, stopped by the Listons' home to wish them happy holidays. Sonny wasn't there. He was at the International. So Powell found himself getting an earful from Geraldine. As he'd later recall to Nick Tosches, Geraldine confided to Powell that she didn't know what to do anymore because "Sonny has gotten unruly."

Unruly. There was another word. After all they'd been through together, it must have taken a lot for Geraldine to call her husband that. It suggested that he'd crossed another threshold, perhaps to a place even she couldn't reach.

13.

___

THE GUTTER

The weeks before New Year's were the one time of year during which the small-town side of Las Vegas came out. The casino executives showed off their families, and celebrities dropped checks on worthy charities as hedonism was put on hold. The showrooms went dark so the show people could rest up for New Year's Eve, and the socialites and clergy briefly took back their town. Amid all the caroling and cater-wauling, the Listons tried hard to act like a family. Keeping to tradition, they visited their friends Davey Pearl and Lem Banker, trading gifts and tidings for the coming year. Banker remembers his friend as being upbeat and optimistic.

Yet at the same time, Sonny was having his loudest, most argumentative meetings with Ash Resnick. According to various accounts, the men were seen almost coming to blows at the Stardust Country Club and huddling intensely at the Thunderbird, possibly to negotiate a separation that would end their milky alliance once and for all.

The backdrop to those meetings couldn't have been coincidental. On Sunday, December 27, the first reports began to surface that Muhammad Ali and Joe Frazier had agreed to fight at Madison Square Garden for the $2.5 million Perenchio and Cooke guaranteed to each. It was crazy money. And Sonny had to have been feeling flush about it. According to an account rendered by the writer Paul Gallender, he called his old friend in Chicago, Barney Baker, and told him that he was about to come through town with $20,000 to repay an old loan. "He said, 'Barney, be at the airport, because from there I gotta be someplace,'" Baker recalled.

Where would he have suddenly gotten $20,000 when he was hustling fifty-dollar bags of coke?

Geraldine was itching to get out of town, possibly so she wouldn't have to see whatever her husband felt that he had to do next. On Christmas Eve she flew to St. Louis to be with her family. When she landed, she called Sonny to tell him she'd arrived safely.

The next day Sonny made a round of calls to family and friends, then bought himself the Christmas Day present of two buxom white showgirls he brought to the Town Tavern on Jackson Street. In a corner booth he spied Clyde Watkins and strolled over to him with the girls. "What are you doin' later?" Watkins asked him.

"Coming to your house to eat," Sonny joked, placing his huge hands on his back.

"He looked like he always looked," Watkins would recall, waiving off any suggestion that his friend was strung-out. "I didn't see much different about him."

To judge from Watkins's recollection, Sonny was feeling good, possibly for the first time in months. Not only was he expecting some kind of windfall, new opportunities were opening up for him in Hollywood.

More than forty years later, a post in a chat room thread would offer a detailed accounting of his next few days. The poster, using an anonymous handle, would recall that Sonny had breakfast on the morning of Monday, December 28, with Pearl at Harry's, a breakfast joint on the east side, at which time they went over plans for him to referee a fight in Japan.

According to the post, Sonny returned home later that morning and called his sparring partner Gary Bates to tell him that he was leaving for Los Angeles but that they should get together when he was back in a couple of days. (In an interview before his death in 2014, Bates confirmed this to me.) In the early afternoon, Sonny set off for L.A. in his new Cadillac.

The anonymous post cited records from Sonny's car telephone as showing that he made two calls to Geraldine, one to Paramount Studios, where he was headed for a meeting, and several to the International. By 8:30 in the evening he'd reached L.A. and had dinner at the Biltmore Hotel with his talent agent. According to what the poster said he was told by the hotel's bartender, the men had their last drink at about 11:30 p.m.

The post also cites "hotel valet records" as showing that the next day Sonny took a cab to Paramount Studios, where he attended a 3:30 meeting with the casting director, Jim Merrick. According to the poster, Merrick's office confirmed the meeting and the studio's front gate logbook showed that it lasted until 5:30 p.m. Sonny then took a cab back to the hotel, where front desk records purportedly showed that he checked out after midnight for the long drive back to Las Vegas.

If the information is true—and it seems too weirdly specific to be made up of whole cloth—Sonny would have been back at his house by the time the sun was rising over the desert on Wednesday, December 30.

At this point the plot thickens, because according to a story that was subsequently printed in the *Sun*, one of the last persons to see Sonny alive was an "undercover narcotics agent" who stopped by Ottawa Drive on December 30.

The story doesn't identify the agent, much less what was said. When I asked Dick Robinson, then the head of the BNDD's Vegas office, what he thought, he replied, "Maybe it was something simple, like a guy just wanted to shoot the shit about boxing." His tone, however, suggested he didn't actually believe that.

"There weren't but ten people who were working drug cases back then," Robinson went on, and he included himself. But he said he wasn't anywhere near Sonny's home on that day, and the BNDD field agent who was working for him, John Sutton, was already back in Los Angeles. Karl Albright, then a sergeant with the sheriff's department who worked closely with Robinson, told me that he didn't visit Liston. And Gary Beckwith, one of the deputies who worked for him, insisted that he wasn't near Ottawa Drive that day and didn't know anyone on the sheriff's force who ever admitted that he was.

There were a half-dozen people on the Las Vegas Police Department who also could have fit the description of an "undercover narcotics agent." But in the end, the candidate who makes the most sense is the one who'd fallen the farthest.

After his humiliating loss to Lamb, there was nowhere for John Sleeper to go but down. Not only was he demoted to a desk job on the graveyard shift, he got demoted again, this time to a mere patrolman. In a few weeks he was going to quit the force to manage a gas station.

It's easy to imagine him stopping by to break the news to Sonny and tell him something like "You're going to be on your own now." But given what was about to happen, maybe there was more to it. Maybe he'd heard something that he felt he had to tell Sonny—something urgent. Sleeper may have been a marked man on the police force, but he still had his ear to the ground. Maybe he'd heard that someone was planning on having Sonny killed

It's not nearly as far-fetched as an undercover narc just dropping by to talk boxing. And it would tie together a lot of loose ends. But whether the secret source was John Sleeper or not, this much is clear: Sonny had a lot to worry about.

He was worried about whether his body could handle another fight and, if not, what he was going to do next. He was worried about his junkie mistress and the drugs they were doing together. He was worried about Red Rodney and Earl Cage and, now that Sleeper was out of the picture, whether he could still count on friendly treatment from the LVPD. He was worried about his gambling debts and his bank account and whether Ali was going to keep his end of whatever bargain they'd struck. When he was sober enough to remember he had a seven-year-old kid, he worried about Daniel and how he was growing up. And, Lord knows, he worried about Geraldine, who worried enough for the two for them. By the afternoon of December 30, Sonny had a great deal of worry on his mind.

There is a famous story that Geraldine would tell about being asleep at her mother's home on December 28 when she was startled awake by a dream. "[Sonny] was falling in the shower and calling my name, 'Gerry, Gerry!'" she told the writer William Nack. "I got real nervous. I told my mother, 'I think something's wrong.'"

But how worried was she, exactly?

As she explained it, she kept trying and trying Sonny without success through New Year's Eve. But despite the fact that she hadn't heard from him in three days, it took her another five days to fly home with Daniel.

Other odd events prevented Sonny from being found. His trainer, Johnny Tocco, claimed that he was excited that Sonny had promised to come to a New Year's Eve party he was throwing at his gym for boxers and their wives instead of a glitzier one that Sonny had been invited to at Caesars. But when Sonny didn't show close to midnight, Tocco said, he called him without getting an answer and tried again at 2:00 a.m. Yet he also didn't seem to be in any rush to get to Ottawa Drive. Instead, the discovery of Sonny had to wait until Geraldine flew home with Daniel on January 5 and stepped into the living room thinking the foul smell that hit her was food left burning on the stove.

"I went in the kitchen and didn't see anything," she'd say. "So I went a few more steps up to the bedroom." And that was when she saw her husband lying against the bed, blood covering an undershirt that barely covered his bloated body.

While no one has ever suggested that Geraldine had anything to do with the death of her husband, in the decades that followed she never gave an entirely convincing account of why she reacted as she did, either. According to a report from the Las Vegas Police Department, she dashed out of the bedroom and drove a half mile to a friend's home, where she "was observed by the people there to be in a very hysterical manner." According to the LVPD, she spent more than ninety minutes trying to reach Sonny's doctor before heading back to Ottawa Drive with her friend.

It was not until 11:00 p.m.—more than two hours after she found the body—that Geraldine finally reached a doctor. And twenty minutes later he was in the Listons' bedroom, looking over the body and confirming what she already knew: Sonny was way past dead.

Geraldine's first call to the police did not come until 11:59. Clyde Watkins says that he heard about it from a friend on the police force not long after. He claims that he grabbed up Joe Louis and Ash Resnick from the floor at Caesars and raced to Ottawa Drive in time to meet the cops.

"Me, Louis, Ash—we all went to Sonny's house," Watkins told me. "Ash drove because I was in shock, and when we got there, there were nine or ten people there, mostly police. Ash and Joe went first and I went behind them. I got to peek up the stairs [as paramedics were lifting Sonny onto a gurney] and I could see Sonny's leg and his arm was all swollen." The men stayed about twenty minutes and then left.

The sheriff's department report makes no mention of Resnick, Louis, or Watkins being at the scene. Craig Lovato, who was part of the first-response team, recalls that three officers—not Resnick and the others—were present when he arrived and that he was directed to the bedroom. "Sonny was loaded up real bad," he told me. "His feet were still on the ground and the gases that built up all went into his penis so it was all swelled up and standing up straight."

Lovato said he looked in the bathroom and found a case of works, leading him to believe that Sonny had shot up and then stumbled back before collapsing backward on the bed. But the overdose theory didn't really gain traction until a detective sergeant identified as S. Lemmon went to the kitchen to use a wall phone and claimed to see something on the kitchen counter: a "small green balloon partially open" with a "white powdery substance."

What's odd about the discovery is that Geraldine had been

in the house for nearly two hours, with ample time to remove anything incriminating. Why would she leave a balloon of heroin out in plain view in the kitchen? The most plausible answer is that she didn't: one of the cops planted it.

Why would they do that? Robinson, the BNDD's Las Vegas station chief, told me that he knew Sonny kept drugs outside the house, in a loose stone in the outdoor fireplace, because one of his informants told him so. Others in the sheriff's department and the LVPD knew it, too. Cops cut so many procedural corners back then, no one would have thought twice about planting a balloon of heroin so they could get a search warrant for Sonny's real stash. It would also explain why Geraldine, faced with this final indignity, didn't lift a finger to help them. "Due to Mrs. Liston's apparent shock over the death of her husband, [we] were unable to interview her for further information," one of the officers wrote.

While the cops were hovering around Geraldine, coroners struggled to get Sonny's corpse from the bedroom to the ambulance below. After they fit it on a gurney, one of the coroners slipped going down the stairs and it went tumbling off. By the time they got outside and started to lift it into their ambulance, a crowd of neighbors began to form. Once again Sonny's weight proved too much, and the gurney tipped over, sending him into a sewer grate.

The patrolman Max Huggins was making his way through the crowd that had gathered when he ran into the neighbor of the Listons who'd previously complained to him about the raucous parties that Sonny threw when Geraldine was away. "I told you he'd wind up in the gutter," she said, snarling at Huggins.

On Tuesday, January 5, the Clark County coroner announced that his official autopsy couldn't pinpoint a cause of death for Sonny. While there could be a link to "possible" needle marks on Sonny's arms, he said, toxicology tests needed to be done before he could be any more conclusive. The *Sun*, with its taste for scandal, cut to the heart of the matter with a blaring headline, "Probe Reveals Liston Possible Narco Victim," and this story:

> The lonely death of former world heavyweight champion Charles "Sonny" Liston, 38, may have been caused by an overdose of heroin, the Clark County Sheriff's Department reported yesterday.
>
> Dept. Capt. Gene Clark said punctures, which may have been needle tracks, were noticeable on Liston's brawny arms. A quarter ounce of heroin in a balloon was found in the kitchen of his home, and a half an ounce of marijuana in the pocket of a pair of pants near his body, said Clark. There was no evidence of foul play, Clark added . . .
>
> An autopsy yesterday did not immediately disclose the cause of death. Tissue and body fluid samples were taken for toxicological and microscopic examination, but these tests will not be completed for several days.

John Sutton was sleeping at his home in Los Angeles when Dick Robinson called him to say, "Your target is gone."

Sutton pulled himself out of bed. He'd seen Sonny less than a month before and the champ looked fine. Better than fine. Fantastic for someone so close to fifty. He thought back to what Sonny had said about heading to L.A. to score drugs. He had plans to go to Vegas in a week and hit up Sonny to make a buy. After that, it was only a matter of time before he'd get Sonny in a room for The Talk.

"Look, I'm not one of your local friends," he'd planned on saying, throwing his badge on the desk in front of Sonny. "This is the federal government. You know what that means? It means I've got you by the balls. It means you're gonna tell me everything you know about who's dealing drugs and who's protecting them, and then maybe we can discuss keeping your ass out of jail."

Or something like that. He figured he had time to get it right. But he'd run out of time. Well, they were busting so many people in Los Angeles that he'd probably stumble on whoever was supplying Sonny. It was just the thrill of facing him down that Sutton missed. At the end of the day, he wanted to beat the champ.

At the funeral on Saturday, January 9, Geraldine was inconsolable. "I can't even see his face. Oh Jesus," she said, rocking back and forth in an anteroom of the chapel behind her husband's silver casket, with Daniel at her side. Then she broke free and screamed, "Can you tell me what happened to you, Sonny?"

It was just the beginning of the strange goings-on over Sonny's lifeless body. The funeral itself was a crush. Between seven hundred and a thousand mourners were trying to get seats in a mortuary that fit four hundred. Joe Louis, one of six pallbearers, was the only heavyweight champion there and came late because, as he explained, he was shooting craps and "Sonny would understand."

According to Lem Banker, Ash stayed away from the funeral because he wanted to avoid questions. There was no sign of Sonny's tall white mistress, although she may have been on the fringes, her junkie eyes hidden under thick mascara and her big breasts covered by the mink coat Sonny had bought her. Sonny's friends from Jackson Street said their good-byes to him over shots at Loves Cocktail Lounge. None of them wanted to be around because they were all afraid they would come under suspicion. But suspicion of what?

The service was conducted by one of Sonny's most ardent believers, Edward Murphy of St. Ignatius Loyola Church in Denver. It had been Father Murphy who'd taken Sonny under his wing a decade earlier, after he'd run into trouble, and watched him train at the Mother Cabrini Shrine. Those inclined to be suspicious of boxing thought of Father Murphy as a "house priest" whose job was to clean Sonny up so he could face Patterson in 1962. But he was earnest and caring and one of the best friends Sonny ever had, and certainly he was the only one to ever say, "Sonny will do very well. I have no worries about him at all. I just have that confidence."

From the dais, Father Murphy gave a moving account of their friendship. "I was able to help Sonny several times," he said, wiping back tears. "I was able to help him so many times that I was criticized by some of my closest friends. I got some praise. I care little for praise, and not at all for criticism. It was my privilege to show my friendship. We should only speak good of the dead: it is a dogma of the Church and Almighty God is all-merciful." He ended by saying: "Sonny had qualities most people don't know about."

After the church ceremony, a procession of Cadillacs followed Sonny's hearse down the Strip. Noticing that the police were escorting it through stoplights, Mike Parkhurst, who'd finished filming the last scenes for his movie, *Moonfire,* turned to Joe Louis and quipped: "Sonny would appreciate we're going through red lights without getting a ticket."

At the gravesite, Geraldine was still so shaken that she stayed in the car, entrusting two of her friends to hold Daniel's hands as he watched the only father he had ever known lowered into the ground. It was a somber moment, but when planes taking off from McCarran Airport drowned out the prayers, Parkhurst turned to Louis again. He'd already scribbled out his own epitaph for his friend—one that would also serve as promotional copy for his movie: "Liston could scowl as hard as any man in or out of the ring. And, of course, he invented the big stare. . . . But

Sonny's humor, warmth and smile, known only to those close to him, come through [on film]. The audience can now share a part of The Man who was all-too-human out of the ring and off the screen."

His capitalization of "The Man" wasn't accidental. He suggested to Geraldine that Sonny's gravestone simply read "A Man," because he felt it summed up all his simplicity and contradictions. His hope that audiences would flock to what he described as Liston's "first and last dramatic role" was a bit optimistic. Still, he felt lucky for the friendship.

"I know why Sonny liked this spot," he told Louis. "From here, he can look up the stewardesses' skirts."

It took until January 19, 1971—precisely two weeks after Sonny's body was discovered—for this press release to be issued:

> Clark County Coroner Mark E. Herman, M.D., ruled
> today that former heavyweight boxing champion Sonny
> Liston died of natural causes and listed lung congestion
> as the immediate cause of death. Dr. Herman . . . said
> the pulmonary congestion and edema was due to proba-
> ble myocardial anoxia or poor oxygen supply to heart
> muscles and a coronary insufficiency, or insufficient sup-
> ply of nutrient blood to heart muscles. "The autopsy and
> microscopic and toxicological examinations failed to
> provide an exact cause of the shortage of nutrient blood
> and oxygen to the heart muscles," Dr. Herman said.

The coroner acknowledged that "traces" of morphine and codeine, the by-products of heroin, were found in Sonny's body tissue. He also conceded that needle punctures "could not be excluded as a cause" of the scars. But he decided that the drugs in Sonny's system were "not in sufficient amounts that could be considered as causing death."

There it stood. The official finding was natural causes.

And it would stay that way until a decade later, when an unlikely figure would come forward with an account that would reveal an even more sordid chapter of crime and corruption.

Part III

CONFESSION

14.

JUNE 14, 1982

I rwin Peters's skin was doused with sweat as he walked into the Las Vegas Metropolitan Police Department, to deliver what he promised himself would be his last confession as a police informant.

Peters scanned the lobby for anyone he knew, but it had been years since he'd traded information for a get-out-of-jail card and this was an entirely new department from the one he'd helped in the early 1970s. As a result of the battle of the badges between the Las Vegas Police Department and the Clark County Sheriff's Department, city officials made the decision to merge the agencies into a single force that would be immune from cross-border incursions and turf wars.

In his younger days, Peters had a minor reputation in Las

Vegas's boxing scene, where he hung around the Silver Slipper and gyms with all other pugs who lived on the margins. His father was a boxer and he knew boxers did a lot of drugs. But he just as easily could have spent his spare time hanging around schoolyards or methadone clinics: the forty-one-year-old informant didn't put high demands on himself.

Walking up to the complaints desk, he announced, "I'm here to report a burglary that's about to take place." Then, watching the duty officer look him over, he added an enticement: "It involves a former cop."

The officer directed him to the waiting area. It was a busy night, which meant it was full of the usual unfortunates: a drunk who'd had his wallet jacked, a woman with a black eye, a couple of college kids who were witnesses to a hit-and-run. And as he waited, Peters reflected for the umpteenth time on where his life had led him. He'd worked hard at being a career criminal. But all of a sudden he was a father of five whose life had become increasingly unmanageable. He needed to get out before someone took him out.

Drumming his fingers, he waited for his name to be called. He was sure that someone would want to hear the story he'd come to tell.

From his gang unit office on the seventh floor of police headquarters, Gary Beckwith could look out over the two dozen officers under his command. One of the unintended consequences of the corporatization of Las Vegas was that it had chased out the old-time mobsters and allowed in a more murderous generation. A pathological killer, Tony Spilotro, made the seventies the bloodiest decade on record when he was dispatched by the Chicago outfit to keep an eye on its Vegas interests, and quickly threatened to kill anyone who didn't pay *him* protection money. Spilotro also led one of the most brazen burglary rings Beckwith had ever seen.

But the mob wasn't even his biggest concern anymore. The Hells Angels were selling meth to schoolkids and the black gangs who sold dope on the Westside had struck an unholy alliance with Mexican dealers who were taking over the desert line. As far as Beckwith was concerned, it was all a symptom of an even larger cancer: Las Vegas was growing too damn fast for its own good. Every time he passed a new construction site, he wondered how much more his city could stand.

With all of that on his mind, he wasn't prepared to get a call at home after midnight from his boss asking him to come back into the office. "Gary, I got a guy I need you to talk with," the head of intelligence said.

"Can't it wait?" Beckwith asked.

"I don't think so. He says he's got information about something about to go down." The head of intelligence paused. "There might even be something in this that's new on Sonny Liston."

Beckwith had been one of the first officers to arrive at 2058 Ottawa Drive when Geraldine reported Sonny's death. Back then he was an undercover deputy who kept his hair in a ponytail and dressed in sleeveless biker vests. When one of his colleagues claimed to have found a bindle of heroin in the Listons' kitchen, Beckwith was the one who was assigned to write the search warrant application and ask for permission to look for "any and all illegal narcotics, namely heroin." The subsequent search hadn't turned up anything. But Beckwith suspected that was because someone had gotten to the drugs before he could.

"Who is it?" Beckwith asked.

"You ready for this?" his lieutenant asked. "It's Gandy. He says he wants to give us Larry Gandy."

It took a moment for the name to sink in. There weren't many cops Beckwith admired. But in the 1960s and early 1970s, Larry Gandy was one of them. Lean, with a pompadour of jet-black hair and blue eyes that could freeze a hundred-degree day, Gandy didn't just take on the toughest assignments. He single-handedly declared war on the Westside.

What Beckwith remembered more than anything was the gimmick Gandy used, because more than a decade later it still inspired awe. In their days on the street, heroin was sold in clear gel caps, usually $120 for a bag of six. Since most dealers wanted their customers to shoot up in front of them to prove they weren't cops, Gandy bought his own capsules and filled them with maple syrup, tucking the placebo pills between his fingers before he went off to an undercover buy. Once he'd bought real heroin, he'd switch the capsules he bought for the fake ones and shoot maple syrup into his vein. It was so utterly bizarre that no one who witnessed him tying off could imagine it was a con.

Before he was pulled from undercover work to save his own life, Gandy had single-handedly set up a hundred perps, maybe more. And the junkies had no idea who or what hit them. They all got dragged into headquarters in handcuffs thinking each had set the other up. In an era when every other cop was either on the take or out of his mind, Gandy was clear-eyed and incorruptible.

But then, suddenly, he wasn't.

All the cops from Beckwith's generation knew the story. In the mid-seventies Gandy had trouble adapting to the newer, more by-the-book era of policing. There were sensitivity classes and lectures about engaging suspects with conversation instead of fists. There were also managers with advanced degrees who'd never spent a day on the street and instead sat in their offices looking at statistics. For Gandy it was heartbreaking to watch cops worry about covering ass instead of kicking it. He was a man lost in another era. And, invariably, it caught up with him.

Beckwith wasn't a hundred percent on the details. Something about a skell threatening Gandy's female partner. Whatever it was, Gandy beat the shit out of the guy and got sued for police brutality. His supervisor demanded that he take a lie detector test and the two got into one of those "Fuck you," "No, fuck *you*" fights. He was fired for insubordination and responded by suing the state in a case that added to his legend. Not only did he win his job back, he won a precedent that gave police officers the same rights as suspects in refusing to take polygraphs. After that, he said "Fuck you" one last time and walked away for good.

As far as Beckwith and every policeman in that building was concerned, Gandy was still a hero.

"Why me?" Beckwith asked his boss.

"Because nobody else wants to touch it," he was told. "Come on. Come in. Figure out if this guy is full of shit."

In the dozen years since Sonny's death, the boxing world had moved on to a new golden age. The much-anticipated "Fight of the Century" between Ali and Frazier was everything it had been expected to be: a vast explosion of technical skill and personal enmity. Over fifteen rounds, Ali failed to answer Frazier's bodywork and went out in much the same way he had come in, hiding behind race when he claimed that his loss was a "white man's decision."

A few months later Ali won the bigger fight when the Supreme Court delivered an 8–0 decision that voided his draft-dodging conviction. In a bid to rid itself of the whole mess, the high court threw out the case by insisting the draft board never adequately explained why it had denied Ali's request for an exemption on conscientious objector grounds. As *The Washington Post* editorialized, "The strange antagonism that many people feel toward Muhammad Ali will certainly not diminish. . . . But now the antagonism must be based on Ali's boxing style. . . . The sincerity of his beliefs and the influence on them by his Black Muslim faith were upheld by the court."

What followed was a carousel of historic (and often histrionic) fights between the three remaining horsemen of the heavyweight division: Ali, Frazier, and George Foreman. In 1973, Foreman beat Frazier with a second-round knockout in Kingston, Jamaica.

In 1974, Ali beat Frazier at Madison Square Garden. Later that year Ali shocked Foreman with an eighth-round knockout in Zaire to reclaim his title. And in 1975, Ali bested Frazier with a fourteenth-round TKO in Manila.

To the extent that Sonny lived at all in memory during that period, it was in relief. Writing about a non-title fight in 1973 between contenders Jerry Quarry and Ron Lyle, a reporter for *The New York Times* suggested, "The ghost of the late Sonny Liston hung over the Madison Square Garden ring last night. But that's all it was, a ghost. . . . The awesome punching power of a Liston was missing, as was [his] frightening sense of evil."

In *The Boston Globe* some years later, Bud Collins called Sonny an ogre and compared him to Genghis Khan and Idi Amin before lamenting, "Ogrehood passed, but wasn't passed on. What did we get for heavyweight champs after Sonny? . . . Not an ogre in the carload. . . . He is an ogre I miss."

Robert Lipsyte, who chronicled Sonny's late-sixties comeback for the *Times*, argued to me, "As time passed, Sonny stayed in the conversation but not as an icon on his own. Eventually, he became part of other people's stories." He was the springboard for Ali, the model for Foreman, the guy who always scared (but never faced) Frazier.

Without a husband to stand by, Geraldine became an almost invisible figure. The woman who'd always been able to shape Sonny's narrative disappeared into the working-class seams of Las Vegas. She went to work as a hostess at the Riviera, hiding her identity behind a nondescript nameplate that read simply *Jerri*. When she did agree to an interview, it was almost always for pay. As she explained to a Spanish-language news crew, "A lot of people said Sonny was paid off [to lose against Ali]. If he was, I wish I'd seen the dollars he was paid."

By June of 1982, most people had settled on the simplest explanation for Sonny's death, which was that he overdosed himself on a heroin bender while Geraldine was away. Certainly that was what Beckwith thought when he drove back to his office past midnight and readied himself for what Irwin Peters had to say.

Peters was already in the middle of telling his story to two detectives when Beckwith arrived at the small interview room. The man he saw was tall and wiry, with red hair that stood on end as if it were magnetized by negative energy. Beckwith nodded to the men to keep talking and pulled up a chair.

Peters was telling the detectives about his background in crime, which started in Mexico when he supported his young family by selling bogus securities to unsuspecting tourists. U.S. authorities collared him, and in exchange for ratting out his friends he got one-way bus tickets to Vegas for his family.

Once they reached town, Peters took a job at an AAMCO transmission shop on West Bonanza that was a way station for small-time hoods who dealt drugs and looked for scams. He chuckled as he remembered the owner of a taxi company who cheated his customers by giving them counterfeit change. Inevitably, Peters wound up running his own cons that got him in enough trouble to land him in the Las Vegas jail.

There he caught the eye of a sergeant who turned him into an informant and assigned him to Gandy. And as they said in the movies, it was the beginning of a beautiful friendship. Despite his red hair, Peters managed to be forgettable enough to rarely make an impression, which made him a great snitch. He'd hear all sorts of things that he passed along to Gandy, some of which helped him make cases and some of which he traded on the street. In return, Gandy was good to Peters. He used John Sleeper's informant budget to give Peters money for tips and kept him on the street long after he should have been locked up.

For the better part of eight years things worked well. And when Gandy quit the police department, Peters assumed they'd go their separate ways. But that turned out not to be the case. Gandy's legal fight against the brutality charges that were lodged against him had been expensive; he'd nearly bankrupted himself fighting them. To dig his way out, Peters said, Gandy flipped the script and did what he knew how to do best: he went back to the streets, this time as a crook, not a cop. In a one-man crime wave, he started ripping off the very same drug dealers whom he used to arrest, by stealing their drugs. Once he got a haul, he'd resell it to the executives he knew in the casinos, the ones who made it their business to supply the high rollers. It was a perfect setup, Peters said. Who was going to complain? Nobody.

Beckwith rubbed his eyes. This guy was already grating on him.

But drugs were just the beginning. Gandy also had a real estate appraiser's license and used his access to houses to case them for burglaries. When Gandy settled on a target, he'd call Peters with instructions to go in first. "I'd go in with a shotgun," he said coolly, showing no hint of remorse. "I'd tell them I'd blow their heads off if they didn't get on the ground." After they were subdued, he said, he'd pull pillowcases over their heads and give

Gandy the all-clear sign. Then his partner would come in and loot the place. Gandy also had a trademark, Peters said. He masked his voice by talking like Daffy Duck.

Beckwith studied Peters, trying to figure out his angle. It was clear that he was angry with Gandy. Over and over again he said that Gandy had cheated him out of a share of their heists. Beckwith found that part reassuring: he always preferred to know someone's motive. But Peters irked the sergeant when he said, "And remember that Sonny Liston thing? Gandy killed him. He shot Sonny up with heroin."

"That's where you lose me, Pete," Beckwith said, making no effort to mask his irritation. "There was no murder. It was natural causes."

Peters waved off the decade-old coroner's finding. "That wasn't an overdose," he said. "It was murder. Gandy bragged about it to me after he did it."

Beckwith replayed the early-morning hours of January 5, 1971, in his mind. Now that Peters mentioned it, he did remember seeing Gandy in the Listons' home. He'd recognized the undercover cop from an incident months before, when they had both been lured to the same house by an informant and nearly got into a shootout. At Sonny's house they'd nodded hello, but that was about it.

Killers often return to their own crime scenes to rubberneck. But every narcotics cop within radio range showed up that night. Gandy's presence didn't mean a thing.

Beckwith looked at his watch. It was one in the morning.

"You said something about a robbery that's going to happen?" he asked, bringing them back to the present.

"Ten o'clock day after tomorrow on East Reno Avenue," Peters answered. "It's a guy we know with thirteen ounces of cocaine in his house. I got it all set up. All you have to do is be there when Gandy walks in."

Beckwith left the room feeling dirty. He hated informants. But he really hated this one. Larry Gandy. Sonny Liston. *Please. . . .*

A fter grabbing a few hours of shut-eye at home, Beckwith returned to the office to dig into Peters's story. He assumed he'd find it was full of holes. But, to his surprise, when he compared the addresses of the houses that Peters said they'd robbed with open cases in the department's files, he found that many of them matched. As he read through the reports, he also noticed one striking similarity: many victims reported that while they were blindfolded they heard the voice of someone who sounded like Daffy Duck.

The more Beckwith read, the more he realized Peters wasn't as easily dismissed as he'd hoped. The problem was his volatility. The guy looked like he couldn't stay sober for a second. That would become an issue when it came time for him to testify before a grand jury. Hoping to keep Peters from going off the rails before he could sort things out, Beckwith assigned a rookie detective named Eric Ducharme to babysit him.

Unlike Beckwith, who found Peters repugnant, the twenty-nine-year-old Ducharme found him likable enough in his own way. As they drove through the suburbs of Vegas, Peters talked about raising three girls and wanting to kick heroin and start a new life. Still, Ducharme doubted he would win any awards for father of the year. At 3:00 a.m. they passed a liquor store and Peters begged the cop to stop so he could buy a fifth of Popov vodka. Ducharme watched as he came back with the bottle, turned it upside down, guzzled it all at once, then wiped his face with a thick-throated "Aaaah."

While Ducharme was reconstructing Peters's confessions, Beckwith worked on the plan to catch Gandy by surprise. According to Peters, Gandy planned to stage the heist early the next day when the target's kids would be in school. Beckwith kept things on a need-to-know basis, making sure only his lieutenant and a few others were aware of what was unfolding. On Thursday evening Gandy called Peters to say that they were green-lighted for ten o'clock the next morning. Beckwith warned the owner of the home, who left town with his family and whatever he presumably kept in his safe.

By the next morning all the pieces of the hastily constructed plan were in place. Beckwith gathered a team of a dozen detectives together and told them that they were going after a decorated ex-cop. As soon as he mentioned Gandy's name, an audible gasp went up. To a man, everyone in that room still considered Gandy a hero. No one could believe he'd broken bad. Perhaps more to the point, they were also frightened of the guy. If it came to gunfire, most believed Gandy would be the one shooting them.

With an hour or so to go—not enough time for word to leak out—Beckwith brought the group to the house on East Reno Avenue. He placed Ducharme in the kitchen with Peters so they could watch from a distance, while outside another half-dozen cops tried to blend into the scenery. Beckwith put himself in the living room, right in the line of fire, with another veteran detective, Cordell Pearson.

Even then, most of the men there didn't believe a robbery was about to go down. They rolled their eyes and shot one another looks that silently said, *Can you believe this shit?* But Beckwith stayed focused. At a quarter to ten he signaled to Peters to call Gandy and tell him that he was in the house. Peters's fingers were shaking as he dialed the number and said, "Hey, it's Pete. . . . Yeah, they're all tied up. . . . It's clear."

At precisely ten o'clock, the handle of the front door turned and a weight lifter's figure filled its frame, blocking the sunlight. The man paused for a moment, getting his bearings.

"Pete?"

"Right here," Peters said, trying to keep a quiver out of his voice.

Gandy took about ten steps into a hallway that led into the living room, then stopped, sensing that something was wrong. Where were the bodies that were supposed to be tied up? And where was Irwin Peters? At that moment he heard the sound of a safety coming off a gun and a voice say, "You're under arrest, Larry."

Gandy's hand dropped to his right side, and for a split second Beckwith was sure the room was about to erupt in gunfire. Pearson, the officer beside him, saw it, too, and yelled, "Get your hands up now!"

"All right, all right," Gandy said, and it was then that the cops saw him throw down what he had in his hands: a pair of rubber gloves he intended on using to clean out the place.

"That was probably the only time in his life that Larry didn't carry a gun," Beckwith would recall. "And we all were grateful to him for that because none of us wanted to shoot him, which we were prepared to do."

Gandy was surprised by his arrest. Despite all the coke he was doing—and he was doing plenty, often with judges and high-profile lawyers—he still considered himself a cautious crook. If he'd straightened out for just a day or two, he would have seen Peters measuring him for betrayal. But he didn't see that. And as a result he'd stumbled into an ambush.

Looking around at the cops, whose faces showed disbelief, he tried to be calm, muttering, "Hey, how ya doing," to a few of them. But his words were met with silence. As Pearson would put it, "We didn't say much, because what are you going to say?"

Under Nevada law, merely walking into the house left Gandy open to a burglary charge. But he wasn't worried. He was friendly with most of the judges in town and had favors coming to him. More worrisome were the *eight thousand* Quaaludes and the ounce of cocaine that he had stashed in his safe back home. Now, that could cause him to do real time. After he was arraigned and remanded to a jail cell, the judge assigned to his case approved Beckwith's request for a search warrant. Fortunately, he made it effective for the next day, giving Gandy a priceless evening to tie up his loose ends.

What followed burnished Gandy's reputation as one fearless motherfucker. He got a bondsman he knew to help him post $16,000 bail and drove to a 7-Eleven that was a block from his house. It was 3:00 a.m. and in the dim glow of the streetlamps he could see that just two cops—Pearson and a partner—were standing watch. Slipping out of the car, Gandy walked in the other direction, taking a desert pathway to a housing tract that led to his backyard. The cops out front had left it unguarded. Moving quietly, Gandy scaled the fence and tried his back door. It was locked. Remembering that the clasp on his son's window was broken, he tried that. It gave way.

Thanks to his bondsman friend, the ex-cop was able to get a message to his wife, Terri, who was sleeping at a friend's house. He needed her to drive up to the front door and distract the cops by causing a commotion. While he was standing in front of his son's open window, he heard a car pull up, and then Pearson shouting, "Stop! Police! Get out of the car!"

With his wife occupying the cops, Gandy slid into his son's room and went to the living room, where he kept a floor safe. He peeled back the rug, quietly turned the dial of the safe until it opened, then scooped the drugs inside into a pillowcase. The lights were on, so he stayed low, confident that his wife would keep the cops busy.

He was about to slide back out when he saw his two German shepherds with their tongues hanging out; they hadn't been fed in hours. He went into the kitchen to put water and food in their bowls. Then he went out the way he had come in.

At daybreak, when the cops were finally able to serve the search warrant, they brought a locksmith to drill the safe open.

Pearson would recall the sick feeling he got upon seeing that it was empty. "I knew we'd been played," he said.

As far as the detectives at Las Vegas Metro went, that put an end to the brief and odd revival of Sonny Liston as the subject of a homicide investigation.

Gandy's crimes, as far as they were concerned, extended no further than burglary and drug possession. There was no reason to jeopardize an airtight serial robbery case with a rumor about a rogue cop secretly killing a famous boxer.

"Look, if we had something substantial as evidence [in the Liston case], we would have gone after it," Beckwith told me years later, when I met him at a casino diner near his home 250 miles north of Vegas, in Ely, Nevada. "Whether we would have gotten a conviction in court or not isn't the point. We would have gone after it."

He pushed aside a cup of coffee he was drinking and looked at me, unblinking. "When I used to make drug cases, I'd be out there risking my neck by myself. One time, I Maced this guy's dog during a raid and a few weeks later I heard he was out and dealing again, so I went back with a different disguise, walked up to the house, and this dog I Maced is barking at me. I knock on a door that's got bullet holes in it and go inside with an informant who tells the guy I'm a relative who needs some stuff, and the guy says, 'God damn it, I just got busted for this shit.' Then he says, 'Aw, hell, all right,' and gives me the drugs. So I left with the drugs, impounded them, and next day we raided him again and took his butt to jail."

He waited for the story to sink in. "And after all that, the case goes to court and a judge lets him off with a misdemeanor conspiracy plea and a fine. I was out there risking my body, my well-being, and that kind of shit happened. My point is: We would have gone after Gandy [on Liston] if we had proof. But all we had was Peters's word, and that wasn't proof. There was no physical evidence, nothing in any police reports that tied Gandy in with ever being involved with Liston. There was nothing but his word. And there was no way we could take it to get any proof."

The obvious question was why he never asked Gandy about Peters's allegations. Beckwith sighed when I asked it.

"There was a time when Larry and I were pretty good friends," he went on. "He dabbled in real estate on the side and I bought some property that he'd listed up in Logandale. I thought he was a good guy and a good cop. But when all of this went down, Gandy got an attorney and didn't want to talk to me. He had a bunch of judges on his side, too. To tell you the truth, he had half of the police department turned against us. Everybody loved him. They loved his personality. And he had some people who were capable of hurting us hating us because of the case we made against him."

Beckwith had been talking for a while and realized he still hadn't answered my question about why he never opened a murder investigation. "We had Gandy on this burglary," he said. "The feeling was: Let's make the strongest case we can against him—and that wasn't going to be Liston. By the time we were done investigating, we'd put together cases on something like three dozen burglaries. We thought we had Gandy for ten years."

He sighed some more. "I have to hand it to him: Larry had a lot of friends who came through when he needed them."

But Peters wasn't finished trying to tie Liston's murder around Gandy's neck. While the burglary case against him was winding its way through the Las Vegas courts, he sent a message to the editors of *Sports Illustrated* insisting that he could help them finger the killer of Sonny Liston.

No other magazine had expended so much ink on Sonny or done it quite so famously. Whether it was Robert Boyle, who peerlessly chronicled Sonny's ties to a "battalion of mobsters, gamblers, front men and hangers-on," or Mark Kram, who once pugnaciously ended a story by calling him a "bum," *Sports Illustrated* threw its best writers at Sonny and let them throw their best punches.

It was no different now that he was dead. Peters's message wound its way to the magazine's chief investigative correspondent, Martin Dardis, who was dispatched to Vegas to hear him out.* Before working as a journalist, Dardis spent many years as

---

*Dardis worked for the magazine until shortly before his death in 2006.

a detective in Dade County, Florida, and he was an expert in getting to the bottom of stories. But a 140-page transcript of the interview he conducted shows that, like Beckwith, he struggled to make sense of Peters's convoluted claims.

Over hours of conversation, Peters took Dardis back to the late 1960s, when he said that he dealt heroin and Sonny was one of his clients. One of his more sensational claims was that the smack was straight out of the evidence locker of the Las Vegas PD.

This might sound far-fetched. But cops and heroin were a big story back then. Writing in 1970 for *New York* magazine, Nick Pileggi observed that "the men who controlled much of [that] city's drug supply, set its price, administered its distribution and ruled its junk trade were a handful of the city's top narcotics detectives themselves." And according to Peters, the evidence room at the LVPD was just as leaky as the one in New York. He claimed his sources gave him the key to get in and a license to load up. "Hell, I've taken as much as an ounce of heroin out of the safe," he told Dardis, before claiming, "I've been to Liston's house about three or four times [to sell it]."

The idea that Peters would have had access to Sonny's home might sound strange, too, except he claimed that the two had known each other for years—since at least 1964, when he said he first met the champ buying heroin at a bar near his transmission shop. After that, the two ran into each other at the Wednesday fights at the Silver Slipper or the gyms around town.

Most important to Dardis, Peters insisted that he also had a personal view of Sonny's falling-out with Resnick, thanks to his friendship with a pair of Vegas cops. As Peters told the story, in the summer of 1970, when Sonny's heroin habit was escalating and Resnick refused to give him any more money, Sonny hired the cops to scare the casino boss into paying up. Their plan was to trail him after he left his office at Caesars and, according to Peters, who said he was invited along for the ride, wait until he pulled up to a stoplight on Eastern Avenue, right by the airport, before firing into the backseat of his cream-colored Lincoln. "I'll tell you one thing," Peters told Dardis, describing what he claimed was Resnick's reaction at having his car riddled with bullets. "You talk about a scared motherfucker."

The story only got more elaborate from there. Peters claimed that after the shooting, the gunman called Resnick to say that it was a message from Sonny and he'd better give the big guy what he wanted. Instead, Peters said, Resnick doubled down by hiring the very same cop to send his own final message. Peters claimed to have been present at a meeting in the parking lot of Caesars Palace when Resnick asked the cop, "What would it cost for us to get rid of Liston?"

This exchange between Dardis and Peters followed:

DARDIS: You're Resnick. You're talking. Tell me exactly what he said.

PETERS: "As heavy as Sonny is using right now, it would be easy to overdose him."

DARDIS: Does he say that before he says, "How much would it take to off Liston?" Tell me what he said.

PETERS: "Do him in."

Peters went on to allege that Resnick paid $25,000 for a batch of pure heroin and that Gandy later bragged about using it to shoot up Sonny.

But the longer Peters talked, the more he peppered his story with qualifiers: He heard . . . He was told . . . He read some-where . . . So much of it seemed secondhand that it was hard to know whether he'd spent the last eleven years keeping a deep, dark secret or whether he was just a professional con man plying his trade.

At the end of the day, no story was ever published, suggesting the award-winning magazine had the same doubts about Peters's story that Beckwith did. But the rumors about Sonny's murder lived on, even after the man who launched them met his own mysterious end.

The postcard arrived at Irwin Peters's home not long after Larry Gandy was taken into custody and then released on $5,000 bail.

The front showed a vista of a barren desert.

The back carried a cryptic note.

"This is where you'll be," it read.

Peters was already afraid for his life, thanks to a strange inci-dent involving his eighteen-year-old nephew. The nephew, who closely resembled him, was visiting Peters's mother—the neph-ew's grandmother—at her trailer in Henderson, Nevada, when the phone rang.

"Is Pete there?" the caller asked, using Peters's nickname. The nephew said no and hung up. A few minutes later, the same caller rang again to ask, "Is Pete there?" Once again the teen said no and hung up. Then he looked outside at the vacant trailer across the street and noticed that there was someone inside, looking his way.

When Peters learned of the incident, he knew he had to get out of town. Every drug dealer he had ripped off already wanted to see him dead. Now half of the Las Vegas PD wanted the same.

"The story I was told was that Uncle Pete worked out a deal where he'd be okay if he stayed out of Las Vegas but all bets were off if he stepped foot in there again," says the nephew, Bradley Scherer, who went on to become a police officer and Nevada state marshal.

Peters moved to Utah and got a job at a car dealership, where he tried to disappear into everyday life. But no matter where he went, the postcard haunted him. He looked over his shoulder, fearing Gandy would get his revenge. "He was really paranoid that Gandy was going to kill him," remembers Eric Ducharme, the former detective.

His drinking got even worse; he divorced his wife of twenty years and lost touch with his kids. The only thing that seemed to brighten his spirits was when he learned that Gandy decided to plead guilty to robbery and cocaine possession and that he'd most likely spend ten years behind bars.

Peters wasn't at Gandy's sentencing in March of 1984. If he had been, he might have had a heart attack right there. After the presiding judge lectured the rogue cop about how he'd disgraced his badge, he imposed a sentence of ten years behind bars, just as

Peters had hoped. But in the next breath, the judge suspended the sentence and let Gandy go free. (There was rampant speculation in the LVPD that the judge was one of Gandy's coke-snorting friends.)

Peters lived like a marked man after that. In 1986 he moved to Grants Pass, a quiet, gated community in Oregon, where he tried hard not to be noticed. He remarried and got another job at a car dealership. Whenever he called his mother in Las Vegas, he warned her not to ask where he was calling from because he assumed her phone was tapped.

On Friday, August 21, 1987, Peters's new wife, Kathi, awoke to hear the couple's car rumbling in their garage. The couple had been married only nine months. When she opened the door she found her husband sitting lifeless in the front seat.

The Oregon Department of Health labeled his death an accident caused by a "leaky exhaust system." But no one who knew the way Irwin Peters lived believed he died accidentally.

As his nephew put it three decades later, "Everyone in our family feels the death was suspicious."

15.

___

SUSPECT NO. 1

Three decades after Irwin Peters's death, all the records involving it seem to have been destroyed or hidden away. The district attorney of Josephine County in Oregon, Ryan Mulkins, spent more than a year scouring his microfilm archives in response to my public records request for any law enforcement documents related to Peters's death. On February 6, 2016, he sent me an e-mail to report: "The sheriff's office informed me that they could not find anything. They think the record was either purged or when the report was photo'd to be put on microfilm the photo just didn't take." The FBI, which interviewed Gandy, responded to another public records request with a letter that stated, "Records which may have been responsive to your request were destroyed on June 29, 1990." And

Peters's widow remains strangely muted about the whole affair. "You're talking about a long time ago," she said when I reached her. "I don't know anything. We weren't married that long."

Wasn't there any detail about him that came to mind?

"Um, no," she replied, rushing off the phone.

When I interviewed Beckwith over breakfast, he didn't come out and directly say that he thought Gandy was involved in Peters's demise. But he didn't have to. For all his feigning indifference about the past, it was clear that he still considered Gandy a stone-cold liar. One episode in particular stuck in his craw.

It occurred in 1985, roughly a year after Gandy pleaded guilty in Las Vegas and got off without jail time. Beckwith spotted the ex-cop driving and pulled him over with a traffic stop. "I went up to him and I says, 'How you doing,' because like I told you before, we used to be friends," Beckwith recalled. "Then I said, 'You really disappointed me, Larry, the way you turned your family and a lot of cops against us on that Irwin Peters case.' That's when he told me, 'I had to do it to save my reputation.' So he admitted it right then and there that he did all we claimed he did, all them dozens and dozens of home invasions."

After he told the story, Beckwith stood up and left a dollar on the table for the coffee he'd ordered. "It really was a spear in my body that he did that to us," he said. "We were just doing the job that he used to do."

The story made me want to know more about the cop who lost his way and what made him lose it. The former Vegas patrolman Max Huggins encouraged me when he mentioned an out-of-the-blue phone call he'd received from Gandy a few months before.

"I hadn't spoken to Larry for years, but he called to say he owed me an apology because I treated him well when a lot of his friends started to ignore him," Huggins said. Gandy's message, he added, was, "I know I screwed up and I've straightened my-self out. I just want to say thanks for talking to me when others wouldn't."

After that, I began to reach out to other men whom Gandy had worked with throughout his career. Pete Beckman, a Las Vegas detective who trained Gandy when he got to the force in 1964, recalled: "When Larry came onto the job I called him Quacker because he sounded like a duck. He had no fear. Every once in a while back then you'd have to straighten a guy out. If a job needed to be done, he'd do it, straight as an arrow."

I asked Beckman what he thought about Gandy's late-seventies criminal turn and he sighed. "It all depends on how you look at it," he replied. "If Larry had started ripping off innocent people, I'd be upset. But he was ripping off scuzzballs."

Joe "the Crow" Crocetti was a newcomer to the LVPD when he was paired with Gandy in 1970. Now a security consultant with a Florida theme park, he told me, "You had to have balls of steel to do what Larry did in the black community. If they knew you were an informant, you were dead. These were bad people and they wouldn't hesitate to kill you and throw your body in the desert. I remember one day he told me to go into some hard place. He said, 'Here, take this gun. I'll be out in the alley. If you have a problem, throw a lamp through the window.' That kind of stuff."

Crocetti went on: "We'd take a radio and a car off the property lot and disappear for, like, a week. Just shack up with a hooker. That's how you did the job back then. There was no rule of law, especially for cops. When I was a rookie riding patrol, I was put with some guys that had been on the job for, like, twenty years, and I'll tell you what, they told you what to do and had no qualms about beating the shit out of somebody if they didn't comply. There was no recourse. That's how it went."

I asked him why he left the LVPD after only five years. "Me and Larry, we became uncontrollable," he replied. "I'd smoke weed every day like you eat breakfast. If I saw some kids smoking, I wouldn't arrest them. I'd just take their shit and smoke it. After five years they made me work in the jail as my punishment. I just finally had enough of it. I got out in '75 and took a job dealing cards in the casinos."

A third partner, H. Lee Barnes, went to work for Gandy in the early seventies when Gandy took a supervisory job on a state narcotics task force. "I was policeman of the year at the Sheriff's Department and had a really solid reputation, but I couldn't take bullshit and I resigned in the middle of some big argument," he told me. "I was working at a place called Griffin Investigations when Larry called. He said, 'I need you up here. These people don't know what the hell they're doing.'

"I liked the idea of working with Larry. But I didn't like his boss. The guy never worked undercover and had no idea what it was like on the street. At that time, we were working a case with a trainee, a woman, and a dope dealer threatened her. Larry confronted the guy. Okay, well, he punched him a few times. You can't do this job and be a Boy Scout. Afterwards, the guy filed a lawsuit and our boss told Larry he needed to take a polygraph. Larry wouldn't do it. So they trumped up some charge and fired him."

I asked Barnes, now a detective novelist, the same thing as the others: What did he think when Gandy went rogue? "We were both very, very poorly treated from all those incidents up in Reno," he answered evenly. "Our names were tarnished, just tarnished. So I think there was probably adventure in it for Larry because he was still going after bad guys. It was just a different way of doing it."

If Barnes holds ill will toward anyone, it's Beckwith. "Maybe what Larry was doing was unethical," he told me. "But I would have gone over to him and said, 'Look, asshole, stop and think about what you're doing. You're trusting a snitch and he's setting you up.' But cops don't cover for one another the way that they once did. Maybe that's better. Maybe it's better for the public, I don't know. Maybe my morality is different than others. But that's how I would have handled it."

There was one thing that Barnes said, though, that stuck with me the most. It came when I asked him which of the two of them—him or Gandy—was more likely to hold a long-lasting grudge.

"Oh, definitely Larry," he shot back. "I didn't mind beating somebody up. But I wasn't going to carry on a vendetta for the rest of my life. The last person in the world I would want tracking me down in those days would have been Larry Gandy."

It wasn't hard for me to track Gandy down.

I used Facebook.

To judge from the photos he'd posted, he certainly didn't look like someone you wanted mad at you. He was about fifty pounds heavier than he was in his police days, and his photos showed him in sleeveless biker vests highlighting biceps that looked like they belonged in a Toby Keith video.

He wore a trim goatee that matched his military buzz cut and even in happy-looking scenes there was very little reassuring about his smile. Still, given what his friends said, it seemed that there was something that wasn't quite coming through in those photos. So I sent him a message: "Since so many years have passed, I'm hoping you'd be open to sitting down with me to talk about your life and career."

Within a few hours, I received this reply:

> I would be delighted to sit down with you. As you know, I was well known in the old days. Some of my activities were positive and some were shameful; however, I have come to terms with my life and realize that I was responsible for my actions. . . . There was a time I would have recoiled at your request but, like I said, I have come to terms with my past. . . .

In a follow-up e-mail, he went on:

I promise you I will be candid and honest with you. I have come to realize over the years that you're remembered for the bad things you have done, not the good. So for clarification you may want me to go into my history as a Las Vegas Police Officer, State Narcotics Agent, Private Detective, Bounty Hunter and all around desperado. I can't justify any of my behavior but can only give you the facts. I know the difference between right and wrong. It should be noted that I have finally forgiven myself and have quit carrying that bag of rocks up the mountain looking for a penance. See you!

We agreed to meet on one of those post-Christmas days in Las Vegas where you can make a few green lights on the Strip and get out of town reasonably fast. I drove past the strip malls that are pushing this city ever farther into the desert and toward the towering cliffs of Red Rock Canyon until I pulled into an airy development. Checking the batteries in my tape recorder, I walked up to the address Gandy gave me.

Before I could ring the bell, the door flew open to reveal a man who looked like Santa Claus in the off-season: roundish and gray-haired with a jolly smile and biker tattoos all over his body. When he held out his hand, he brimmed with genuine enthusiasm.

I'd prepared dozens of questions but he didn't let me get to any of them. Instead, Larry Gandy wrapped his thick arm around me and said, "So, you've come to ask me if I killed Sonny Liston."

H e led me into a loft office with framed newspaper clippings on the wall. Unlike the other cops I'd spoken with, Gandy didn't seem to be in any hurry to leave his past behind. One article on the wall was about the war he had waged on the Westside's drug dealers. Another chronicled the three-year fight he had carried on to clear his name against brutality charges in the mid-eighties.

"I've been living with this for thirty years," he said. "It's time to get some things straight."

Gandy started with his childhood in Bryan–College Station, Texas. "I grew up on a farm and I always liked dogs," he said, "so I got into handling canines. In '63, I volunteered to fight in Vietnam and they sent me to Thailand to help clear out an area in Phuket," which the Air Force wanted to use as a staging ground for missions into Vietnam. "I got the first kill at Phuket. In one night alone I killed a VC. We were side by side. And that's what fucked me up and gave me PTSD. I killed a guy at four feet. When you look somebody right in the eyes and pull the trigger on them it's hard on you."

He was young and handsome then, with a snarky smile that oozed confidence, but after that moment a change came over him. His deep-set eyes could sparkle one second and go dead the next. "After I finished my tour, I came to Vegas, where my mother was living, and got work as a canine officer," he went on. "It was great. I had the run of the city until one day I'm flying down West Charleston and another car runs a stop sign. I left two hundred ninety-seven feet of four-wheel skid before impact. Then I went backwards sixty-seven feet. My dog went ape shit. He wanted to eat me. I hit so hard, the engine [was] in the front seat with me."

While he was on desk duty, Gandy began hanging around the casinos, doing the odd security job. One day, Redd Foxx asked him, "You know how Ike Turner saved my life?"

"No, how?" he bit.

"He got me off heroin and onto cocaine."

Another day a detective walked by him while he was still on desk duty and asked, "Hey, kid, you got any balls?"

"Yeah, probably got more than you," he answered.

And that's how he got into narcotics, he told me, sitting back in his recliner. "Nobody wanted to go over to the black side and work heroin dealers. But I had no problem with it. In fact, I became such good friends with one of them that I got groceries for his children out of my own pocket."

The problem for Gandy wasn't getting introduced to dealers. It was what he did once he was alone with them. The heroin addicts he pursued routinely asked their customers to shoot up to prove they weren't cops. He described that trick he had come up with—sticking gel caps laced with maple syrup between his fingers and switching them out after he made an undercover buy with the ones he'd just bought that were filled with heroin.

"I'd put them in there with water, cook it up, tie off and shoot [the concoction] into my vein. Then I'd put on my sunglasses and just sit back and watch everybody while I acted like I was nodded out. Guys would ask, 'Hey man, what do you think of the drugs [he'd pretended to shoot]?' And I'd say, 'This ain't shit.' I've had guys literally overdose on their fucking own drugs because I was so convincing. They couldn't believe I didn't like their stuff. They'd be saying, 'I know this is good shit,' and then tie off and go, 'Ooohh.' I'd have to walk them out because you couldn't just leave them to die. So I'd be walking them around, trying to save their life and all this crap. My lieutenant used to say, 'You scare me to death.' But that was my gimmick."

I glanced at the clock. We'd been together for twenty minutes and he'd already covered killing a man at point-blank range, getting into a head-on car crash that nearly ended his life, and posing so convincingly as a junkie that he nearly caused real junkies to overdose.

And all of that was just a prelude to a story about the man who ended up dead after inadvertently following Gandy's wife around town.

Gandy was careful about keeping his cover. But Vegas was still a small city and every so often shit happened. One afternoon it happened when a pair of drug dealers he knew from the West-side drove past his suburban home while he was watering his yard and recognized him. Figuring he was just another husband hiding a degenerate second life, one yelled out to him, "Hey, let's go get some drugs." Not wanting to break character, Gandy ran into his house, told his wife to dial the vice squad, and then left to join the men.

Even though the episode passed without incident, Gandy worried that his cover might be compromised. So he came up with a scheme that would blend the story into his narrative. He had two uniform officers chase him through the Westside as he drove the same car that the dealers had seen parked in his driveway—a bright orange Dodge—until they all screeched to a halt right in front of the Town Tavern on Jackson Street. With a crowd gathering around them, the uniform cops pulled Gandy out of the front seat and threw him to the ground so they could cuff him. "The part where they beat the shit out of me was their idea." He chuckled as he told the story.

The ruse worked well enough for Gandy to remain undercover and rack up evidence for dozens of arrest warrants. When he couldn't go any further, the LVPD pulled the plug on his one-man operation and deluged the Westside with officers to make mass arrests. As Gandy was sent to work on another undercover operation on the Strip, one of the dealers who had seen him watering his yard put two and two together. Once he figured out that Gandy was the source of all the arrests, he started tailing the cop's Dodge, sending an unmistakable message that the two of them weren't done with each other. The problem was that Gandy wasn't behind the wheel. His wife was. When she noticed she was being followed and called her husband with the plate number, he went berserk. He ran the number, found out who was doing the tail, and sped to the Westside on a tear. By his own account, he stormed into bars, into junkie hideouts, even a Nation of Islam mosque, screaming the name of the hood who'd dared to follow his car. By the time he finally found who he was looking for, the guy was slumped on a corner, dead of an overdose.

Gandy surmises that an overlord who wanted to avoid a war with the cops killed the dealer as a peace offering. "I felt terrible, because I didn't want to kill the guy," he told me. "I just wanted him to leave me the fuck alone. But anyway, that's how that goes."

Gandy left the police force in 1974 to work as a private investigator and a bounty hunter, pursuing the same drug dealers he used to bust, but this time for profit. On the force, he knew cops who helped themselves to a share of the drugs they seized; however, he insists he never crossed that line in uniform. But as a civilian, suddenly he was free to do anything he pleased. Using bail bondsmen he knew to get tipped off when a high-grade trafficker got arrested, he'd barge into their empty homes and loot all the drugs he could. Then he'd sell them to clients in the biggest casinos, most of whom were either hooked or trying to hook high rollers. "I can't name the people who were buying from me back then because they're still alive," he told me. "But trust me, they were big names."

He became the ultimate rationalizer, convincing himself that by furnishing his well-heeled friends, he was still taking drugs off the street. Yet in all of this, the only thing his former colleagues didn't understand—the only thing!—is why he refused to cut ties with Irwin Peters.

"My biggest surprise," Lee Barnes had told me, "was that Larry would ever trust a snitch. I remember having breakfast with him one day and this Irwin Peters shows up. He'd just come from Utah and he says to me, 'I got a problem in Salt Lake with this guy. Would you come up there and beat him up?' I didn't know if it was a setup or what, but I called Larry that night and said, 'That guy's wrong.'"

I asked Gandy to tell me his version of how they met. "Pete

was able to talk," he said. "He told you these stories that would make your head spin. He told a bunch to my sergeant, who decided to make him an informant. The first time I met Pete was on the second floor of police headquarters, where we had the holding cells. I loved my job, so I'd deal with anyone. If I knew what was in store, I would have run for the desert. The guy was a snake. He could produce cases because he hung out with thugs. But he played people."

In his statements to police, Peters insisted that Gandy called him every time he found someone new to rob, and by the early eighties they'd racked up fifty heists. But although Gandy admitted as much to police, he denied that to me, saying he'd gone along with Peters's exaggerations because the cops were threatening to throw his wife in jail as an accomplice. "There were quite a few, but there hadn't been no fifty," Gandy said. "I made up shit to get my wife free because they were going to book her."

By this point I'd lost track of the number of crimes Gandy had admitted to committing, in and out of uniform. The most fateful one, though, was the heist on East Reno Avenue that Peters set him up with. After he bonded out of jail and tricked his pursuers by cleaning out his safe, he tried resuming his life selling real estate even though he had an indictment hanging over him. Not long after, he said, Peters came to his real estate office yelling and waving a .38 caliber handgun wildly. "I guess he was going to shoot me," Gandy said with a shrug.

Gandy, I noticed, gained energy as he told the story and the blood of the old days coursed again. But he became strangely coy when I asked him what had become of Peters after he fled

Las Vegas. The ominous postcard of the desert that the snitch received carried the signature of someone named Bandit, which was a handle that Gandy sometimes used. That didn't mean he sent the card. Someone could have sent it pretending to be him. Still, it did add to the suspicion around him, especially after a Las Vegas Metro homicide detective came to visit.

"He asked me, 'Did you kill Irwin Peters?'" Gandy recalled. "I said, 'Did he have every bone in his body broken? No? Well, then I didn't kill him.' Even my mom sent me the obituary on a piece of cardboard with a flower drawn next to it. I went, 'Oh my God, my own mother!'"

He laughed a laugh that didn't end so much as trail off in a long, mirthful wheeze. "You want to know who I think did it?" he asked.

It took me a second to realize he was talking about Sonny Liston and not Irwin Peters. Before I could get my bearings, he said, "I'll tell you who. It was Earl Cage."

The beauty shop owner. The Westsider who'd been selling heroin out of his back room in between sleeping with his clients. The subject of the federal raid that almost left Sonny shot before the local cops released him into the night.

As Gandy leaned backward, calm as could be, it suddenly struck me that this was the reason he had invited me into his home. He'd spent the last thirty years trying to outrun Irwin Peters's allegations. Now, while he had a chance, he wanted to offer up his own suspect. A dead beautician.

"Everybody needed to go to jail that night," he said. "But they didn't. One guy was let go. Sonny. And a low-mentality individual will think only one thing: The guy who was let go is a snitch."

He let his theory hang in the air. Cage had concluded that Sonny set him up. And in return, he took a contract out on Sonny's life.

According to the Social Security Death Index, Earl Cage died in Louisiana in 2000. His son, Earl Jr., died in 2012. So no one will be rushing to defend him against a decades-old allegation that he killed a heavyweight champion. Still, Gandy seemed certain that he'd solved the crime. If Sonny wasn't an informant, the mere fact Cage believed he was could have been enough to kill him.

As I got up to stretch from my conversation with Gandy, I noticed it was two hours since I last looked at the clock. He'd kept me spellbound the whole time. As we said our good-byes, I realized how he'd managed to deceive so many people for so long. He'd done terrible things. And selling stolen drugs to degenerate casino bosses was the least of them. He'd turned half of the Las Vegas PD against Beckwith—a good cop who was just doing his job. But even when Gandy was hitting rock bottom, turning into a cocaine addict and a crook, he never lost his sense of the absurd.

His friend Lee Barnes became the writer. But Gandy had the keener sense of drama. He'd turned himself into the biggest character of all.

16.

THE WRONG GRAVE

These days the Moulin Rouge on West Bonanza is the same overgrown magnet for vagrants and junkies that it was when Sonny wheeled by it in his pink Cadillac. A fire ravaged the hotel about ten years ago and the city has been at war with preservationists to knock it down ever since. In 2014 a New York investment group bought the hotel site as part of a bid to open a $250 million complex that it hopes can draw traffic from new development downtown. But the chasm between that hope and reality is still stark. To keep their gaming license, the owners had to put a trailer on the fifteen-acre site and let a few blue-haired ladies pull slot machines for an afternoon.

Jackson Street, too, seems stuck in its worst days. A Nation of Islam mosque stands stoic sentry over what used to be a rollicking world of music and unhinged desire. Out front, bow-tied men offer grim-faced warnings to anyone who lingers along the vacant boulevard, which is mostly marked by bail bondsmen and boarded windows.

A mile away, Tony Hsieh, the San Francisco–bred billionaire who wasn't even born when Howard Hughes was buying up the Strip, is trying to create an open-air city out of the abandoned buildings downtown that once served as a glorious gateway to Glitter Gulch. He's pouring $350 million into high-rise apartments and tech-friendly office space using Silicon Valley lingo to talk in terms of a start-up city. As one executive blogged: "Imagine if Walt Disney ran Silicon Valley but everyone lived on the set of *Cheers*."

In this atmosphere, the only history that Las Vegas has room for is the kind that fits under polished glass and recessed lighting. The Mob Museum, which opened in 2012 in the old federal courthouse on Stewart Avenue, curates a century of homicides into exhibits that are ready-made for school outings and, remarkably, weddings. ("The Mob Museum is Las Vegas' most arresting venue," its website boasts in a section dedicated to event planning.) Not far away, the open-air Neon Museum allows visitors to walk through a graveyard of old hotel marquees, including the one for the Moulin Rouge. On one visit, *New York Times* architecture critic Edward Rothstein remarked: "You want stardust? Here it is."

Amid all this processed nostalgia, no one really wants to remember Sonny Liston the way he was in his last days: strung-out on junk and pouring drugs into the bloodstream of a sick neighborhood.

In a feel-good ceremony at Caesars Palace in August 2014, the Nevada Boxing Hall of Fame inducted Liston into its "Home of Champions" with a sepia-toned slideshow and loving testimonial from a social services worker from Philadelphia who has claimed in interviews to be one of Sonny's illegitimate children. When I talked to William Wingate, he remembered Sonny as a gentle giant who used to bring him ice cream and take him for rides in his Cadillac. "He'd come by and hold me and say, 'Are you all right? Are you okay?'" Wingate told me. "It wasn't until I was in my twenties that my mother told me that was my father."

The temptation is to turn all of this into a requiem for a heavyweight—a sad story about a champion who didn't know what to do when the cheering stopped. And it's true that, after a lifetime of beatings from the press and the public, Sonny was profoundly insecure. He was so insecure, in fact, that he fell back on the only thing besides boxing that he'd ever done well: crime. But let's be honest. He also got plenty of breaks along the way. As much as he was harassed early in his career, he was coddled later in it. The Vegas cops cut him more breaks than he had a right to expect. The only thing they didn't give him was a homicide investigation.

Craig Lovato, who found the set of works in Sonny's bathroom, discounts the idea that he was killed in a violent struggle. "Finding the kit right there in the bathroom, the only thing that made sense to me was that he shot up, stumbled backward, and collapsed there on the bed with his feet still on the ground," he says. Still, the veteran agent acknowledges that an accidental overdose might not be the whole story. "If it was foul play, the people who sold it to him knew it was a hot shot," he told me.

Others are less equivocal. "Knowing Las Vegas like I did, and knowing Sonny's history, I always felt he was murdered," says Bill Alden, the BNDD agent who was part of the Earl Cage raid and later rose to the very top of the Drug Enforcement Administration. "There was just too much there."

It's hard not to keep returning to the image of Geraldine throwing herself at her husband's casket and asking, "Can you tell me what happened to you, Sonny?" Whatever she found in their home hadn't satisfied her skepticism about the manner of his death. An accidental overdose? It was too pat, too convenient.

Obviously, the first step should have been finding out where Sonny got the heroin that he injected. But thanks to the conclusion of the Clark County coroner, Mark Herman, investigators never took that step.

Herman wasn't an expert in pulmonary disease. Far from it. But after studying toxicology reports, he concluded that Sonny had died from a rare malady called Syndrome X, in which someone with perfectly healthy large blood vessels has small ones that are inflamed. As the writer Nick Tosches has noted, women and diabetic men tend to get it most. It was almost unheard-of for Syndrome X to be diagnosed in a non-diabetic adult male like Sonny.

It's worth noting that Herman had been in his job only a few months when he was asked to render the conclusion. And while not a political employee, he wasn't exactly immune to politics, either; Herman, formerly an assistant health officer, stepped into the job when the county's top health officer, Otto Ravenholt, resigned to run for Congress in the 1970 elections.

Yet Herman forged ahead with his finding, dismissing the heroin metabolites that were found in Sonny's blood in favor of the more exotic diagnosis. He focused on an "an increase in fibrous tissue" in the small blood vessels going to Sonny's heart and surmised they caused a shortage of oxygen to the heart, or a "*probable* myocardial anoxia," which triggered his lungs to fill up with fluid. Lung congestion was ruled as the "immediate cause of death."

At least one enterprising cop, however, wasn't so sure. On January 20—the day after Herman's report was released—a lieutenant who worked on the sheriff's department homicide squad paid a visit to the doctor who treated Sonny after his Thanksgiving Day accident. According to a copy of his report, he asked the doctor, Richard Browning, what he thought of the coroner's conclusion. Could Sonny have died of natural causes "without some other contributing factors"?

Browning explained that the EKG tests he did on Sonny showed that the massive impact of the crash had caused "a contusion to his heart." His patient had shown such "considerable improvement" during his hospitalization, however, that Browning seriously doubted that contusion could have been the sole reason for Sonny's death. If Sonny's "improvement had continued at the expected rate, [his] heart would have been in a condition not to have resulted in death without other contributing factors," Browning told the lieutenant.

Nonetheless, Herman's ruling stood. And with that bit of postmortem misdirection, the acting coroner single-handedly ended the prospect that Sonny's death would be investigated as a homicide.

There's no way now, more than four decades later, to trace that heroin back to its source. But instead of asking who had access to the heroin that killed Sonny, the better question is: Who had access to Sonny?

Maybe Gandy is onto something with Earl Cage. He had a vicious temper, a long memory, and an intense hatred for snitches, which would have led him to keep returning to the evening in February 1969 when everyone in his home was arrested by the feds and hauled off to jail. Everyone except Sonny.

Gandy argues that singular act signed Liston's death warrant. "I was careless once and one of my snitches got killed as a result of it," he told me. "So I've always been very guarded about how I act with them. I think Earl Cage put out the contract. But John Sleeper was the one who got him killed. See, Sleeper was a great guy, real nice, but he was in way over his head. You can't do what he did. You can't let just one guy walk out. Everybody's got to go to jail."

A story that appeared in the *Sun* in the fall of 1970 plays into this revenge theory. It involved a drug trafficker who'd been convicted of slaying a police informant and given the death penalty. As it happened, the inmate was innocent and got released after the real killer confessed. But the underlying murder of an informant sent chills through the Vegas underground. As a narcotics officer told the *Sun*, "The murder made it very difficult to get informants to work for us in West Las Vegas."

Of course, by heaping suspicion on the beautician, Gandy conveniently takes it off himself. There's also the issue of timing: the raid occurred nearly two years before Sonny's body was found. That's a long time between insult and injury. Why would Cage have waited two years to go after Sonny?

"See, that's how they get you," Gandy explained coolly. "They always wait a little while so there's no suspicion."

R obert "Red Rodney" Chudnick, the criminal trumpeter, was one of the small handful of people who could have gotten in to see Liston.

True, he'd recently been staying away. With Ava Pittman on trial and the federal BNDD raising its profile, he feared that Sonny might make the kind of mistake that could send them both to prison. Despite all that the men had been through, it wouldn't have taken much for Chudnick to drop by and give the junkie his final fix.

A couple of things, specifically, raise Chudnick's profile as a suspect. According to Mark Rodney, one of his dad's crew members had recently sold drugs to a client who overdosed. That suggests he had some pretty powerful heroin on hand. The bandleader also had a way of sneaking in and out of Sonny's house unnoticed. As Mark remembers, he'd visit a neighbor who lived down the street, go out the rear door, and snake along the golf course until he got to Sonny's home unseen.

Red, according to his son, was unemotional when he heard that Sonny had passed. He crinkled his face and said, "I told you the idiot would kill himself." He seemed more upset about the two men in suits who visited the house soon after. Mark assumed they were cops. "They asked me for my dad and stuck their feet in the door so I couldn't close it," he recalled. "When I went to get my dad, he gave me all the drugs we had in the house and told me to bury them in the backyard."

If that heroin had been tested, what would it have shown? Chudnick wasn't going to give the cops a chance to find out. Rather than risk answering their questions, he left town for a while, telling his son to get rid of whatever they had left. Eventually, Chudnick suffered a stroke that left him unable to play. But teetering on bankruptcy, he was able to turn his life around in the early 1980s by rediscovering jazz, and he had a late-life renaissance a decade later as a teacher at Berklee College of Music in Boston.

Mark, who'd found his own fame on the West Coast in the early seventies as half of the light-rock duo Batdorf & Rodney, remembers having dinner with his father shortly before he died in May 1994. Over the meal, his father leaned in and told him, "If things back then were like they are today, we would have been goners."

Ash Resnick was Sonny's gateway to the good life. From the moment he waited for Sonny on the tarmac of McCarran Field in his Thunderbird in 1962, he was the player, the fixer, the hookup. Not only did Resnick help Sonny give up his title in Miami, he may have convinced him not to win it back in Lewiston. Sonny thought that in return he was going to get a cut of Ali's future earnings—a payday that was about to pay off in the winter of 1970. But no one else seemed to agree.

Irwin Peters alone popularized the idea that Resnick was involved in Sonny's demise.

Even the FBI, which was willing to listen to the conspiratorial ravings of a manic-depressive swindler like Barnett Magids, found the idea too preposterous to open a case file on it.

In fact, Resnick's defenders think it's highly improbable that he ever would have met someone like Peters in the fragmented social orbit of Las Vegas. Resnick was at the top of the most fashionable resort on the Strip. He wined and dined his friends in the Bacchanal Room and dropped tens of thousands of dollars on craps. Peters was a twitchy alcoholic who worked at a transmission shop.

Still, Peters was able to weave the story about being in the middle of a war between Resnick and Liston in the waning days of 1970, when, he said, Sonny needed money to support his heroin habit and was badgering Resnick to give it to him. Peters claimed that when Resnick refused, Sonny hired Peters and

Gandy to shoot up Resnick's car as he left Caesars one night. "Talk about a scared mutherfucker," Peters told Martin Dardis. And he was able to drag Gandy into the middle of it. According to the transcript of his interview with Dardis, he claimed Gandy was the cop who fired the shots into Resnick's Lincoln when he was stopped at the traffic light.

Gandy emphatically denies being the shooter, and denies the next chapter in Peters's story: that Resnick called them to a meeting in the parking lot of Caesars to hire them himself with this suggestion: "As heavy as Sonny is using right now, it would be easy to overdose him." Sliding toward me, Gandy said, "The only people I've ever killed in my life were in Vietnam and I'm still paying for them."

Give Peters credit. As implausible as his story might be, he had an uncanny ability to get people to listen to it, not least because he was shrewd enough to make it sound familiar. Take the part about him being in the backseat of Gandy's car when they shot up Resnick's Ford LTD. That seems to be appropriated from a 1974 story in which an unidentified assailant opened fire on Resnick's Ford with a .38; not long afterward Resnick found sticks of dynamite under his car. As Frank Sinatra once joked, "Ash said he'd lend me his car the other day, so I went out and rented one."

Resnick also had reason to be concerned about Sonny's reckless behavior. The FBI was crawling all over his casino, and the $2 million it seized from the secret deposit boxes of top executives was just the beginning. An FBI memo from the period called Caesars "a front for some of the most notorious fixes and swindles in the history of sport" and concluded about Resnick: "To break AR would bust the entire place open and flush out the last of the mob cancer. He is vulnerable as there are too many weak links."

If Resnick had even a hint that Sonny was the subject of a federal drug investigation, or that he was hedging his bets as a part-time informant for the Las Vegas PD, he might have concluded that Sonny was one of those weak links.

It's a long way from that to surmising that Resnick commissioned a hit. But it's not so long as some would suggest. He knew how to play the odds. At a minimum, Resnick might have pulled his protection of Sonny, freeing someone else to do the job.

After my long interview with Gandy, I decided that the man was impossible not to like. But as I said good-bye to him and walked into the fading Las Vegas afternoon, I also had to remind myself that dead bodies had a way of collecting around him.

In late 1970, Gandy was a hero cop who by his own admission had come back from Vietnam so mentally scarred that the only way he could cope was by doing suicide runs into the worst drug precincts of Las Vegas. He took chances no one else would take. He lived among junkies. And he had access to the strongest smack on the street.

During the most self-destructive period of his life, he turned to crime, only to get turned in by the otherwise irredeemable Peters. "If I'd never started doing drugs, I wouldn't have ever got caught and then I'd probably still be a thief," he told me. "The best thing that ever happened to me was getting caught."

Gandy has a gift for putting people at ease and a belly laugh that goes on and on. Best of all, he can laugh at himself, which is an endearing trait. Yet between the belly laughs come remarks that stop you cold. Like when he says he doesn't answer his phone because that's "kept me alive all these years." Or when he wonders why people were ever scared of him and then quotes a friend as saying, "Because you wanted them to be afraid of you, Larry. You were scary."

Gandy also speaks in the kind post-traumatic stress group lingo that helps people distance themselves from their pasts. But there's no unseeing what he's seen. Like a small knot of other cops who try not to look back, he was a witness to an era when Las Vegas was torn apart by race, heroin, and corruption on its police force. It's the same world that Sonny lived in, which is why Peters's allegations about Gandy hover over the Liston case.

It's not beyond belief that Peters and Gandy stole heroin out of the leaky evidence room at LVPD headquarters, or that they sold it to Sonny. Gandy even admits to being a drug dealer. It's just a question of when he started. Did he wait until the mid-seventies, when he left police work in disgust? Or did he begin earlier than that? Maybe five or ten years earlier?

Gandy, of course, insists he was always a clean cop. And he claims to have met Sonny only once, in a chance encounter outside Friendly Liquor Store, and that he never sold him heroin. He also has an alibi for the period when Sonny died: he said he was with his partner on the LVPD, Joe Crocetti.

Crocetti confirmed that they were on one of their weeklong benders when they learned that Sonny was dead. "We heard a call for narcotics detectives to come to Ottawa Drive," Crocetti told me. "I stayed in the kitchen with a couple of other detectives while Larry walked in the bedroom. The whole thing lasted five minutes and we just went on our merry way." Lapsing into mockery, he added: "If Larry [killed Liston], he did it while he was with me and two hookers, and we had a big party while we were doing it."

In the realm of airtight alibis, being on a weeklong acid trip with a hooker in a dingy motel isn't exactly *Perry Mason* material—especially coming from a witness who admits he was once able to "smoke my weight in weed."

But I would have felt more comfortable about it if Gandy hadn't added his own curious detail: After he left Liston's home on January 5, 1971, he visited Irwin Peters. "I told him how horrible it was seeing that body," he confided. "You know, when it's somebody you've admired over the years, it's pretty traumatizing."

I found it hard to believe that, with all he'd seen, looking at the body of a dead heavyweight would be traumatizing. The man had chased a heroin dealer to his death, killed at close range, and done enough blow to bend himself backward. Seeing Sonny's bubbling body during a hooker-and-weed bender should have just been another day at the office. But even more disconcerting was that he felt the need to tell Peters about it. Maybe it was as innocent as he said. Maybe he just casually mentioned it to his snitch and Peters blew it out of proportion by doing what con men do: weaving a little strand of truth into a big lie in an effort to set Gandy up for a fall. But the little details weren't adding up.

There's one last piece of the puzzle that's never been adequately explained. It's a strange story that appeared in the *Sun* on the day after Sonny was discovered: "Narco Agent Last Person Known to Have Seen Sonny Liston Alive." The story read:

> The last person known to see Sonny Liston alive was an undercover narcotics agent. Sheriff's detectives said yesterday Liston, known as the "bad man" of professional boxing, was visited at his home Dec. 30 by the agent. They refused to divulge the nature or reason for his visit but did say Liston was apparently in good health at that time.

I'd come up empty trying to find the mysterious visitor on my own. Dick Robinson, the BNDD agent, said it wasn't him, just as his two colleagues from the era, Bill Alden and John Sutton, did. Karl Albright, a sheriff's sergeant who worked closely with them, said he hadn't been near the place, as did Gary Beckwith, who worked under Albright in those days. Beckwith said he hadn't heard of anyone in his department who had.

"I can tell you this," Crocetti told me when I showed him the story, which he said he'd never seen. "If somebody visited him before his death, it wasn't me or Larry, because we were busy. We were busy. Honest to God."

My personal choice for the mysterious visitor is John Sleeper, who died in 2004 at the age of seventy-seven. Once he'd risked everything on his ill-conceived campaign for sheriff, Sleeper couldn't have protected Sonny from a parking ticket. But he still had his ear to the ground. Maybe he heard something that made him think Sonny was in danger. Maybe it was bad enough that he felt he had to come to Sonny's house to warn him in person. "Sonny, I can't help you anymore, but you have got to watch out for . . ."

When I ran that idea by Crocetti, he waved it off. He was so eager to implicate Irwin Peters that he argued, "I don't believe it could have been Sleeper. It sounds like Peters was the one. He was the one that could get in there to visit Liston. If Liston wanted heroin he could have gotten it from Peters, who wouldn't have had qualms about killing anybody. He could have gone to the guy [and said], 'Hey, look, I've got this great dope,' and then overdosed him. How's that for a fucking story?"

Pretty good. But maybe the truth lies somewhere in the middle. Sleeper knew Peters from the snitch's work as an informant for the LVPD. Maybe he'd heard something about Peters taking a contract that he felt he needed to share.

It's just a theory. But it would tie together some loose ends. Irwin Peters takes a contract to kill Sonny by giving him some pure-grade smack. Maybe the contract came from Earl Cage. Maybe it came from Ash Resnick. Who knows? But just before Peters can pull it off, John Sleeper, in a final act of fidelity, comes to Sonny's house to warn him. "Sonny, I can't help you anymore, but you have got to watch out for . . . *Irwin Peters.*"

———

In the end, Irwin Peters tried and failed to hang Sonny's death around the neck of Larry Gandy. But he wasn't crazy. As a creature of his city, he understood how deals got made, debts got paid, and lives got taken. His story may have suffered from having an implausible ending. But it's foolish to dismiss its period-piece details: the cops who were on the take; the judges who were on coke; the casino bosses who dealt drugs as well as cards; and the fading fighter who couldn't see what everyone else in Vegas did—a problem who needed to go into the ground.

All these years later, the immediate cause of Sonny's death seems plain enough: he shot himself up in his bathroom, stumbled backward in his underwear, and collapsed on his bed. But it's what happened afterward that turned a seemingly accidental overdose into something suspicious. Over the next week, as methane was building up in his body and his skin was beginning to bubble, no one seemed concerned enough about the champ's disappearance to investigate it or even apparently knock on his door. It was a sign of how thin his friendships were and how uncertainly he'd been clinging to life.

Of course, that was a sign of how Las Vegas operated in that era, too. Before cell phones and twenty-four-hour surveillance cameras, everyone disappeared at one time or another. Howard Hughes did it. Frank did it. Even a hero cop like Larry Gandy could vanish for days on end—shacked up with his dopehead partner and a couple of hookers in a dingy motel room—without raising questions.

What's strange is that Geraldine would wait until five days after New Year's to come home when she hadn't been able to reach her husband. Maybe she just assumed Sonny was on one of his benders. But there's also the lag between when she finally got home on January 5 and when she called the cops: that three-hour missing window when she drove to a friend's home and then returned to her place. What did she find there?

A more thorough investigation would have pursued that, as well as where Sonny got the heroin he injected. The house could have been dusted for prints. The Westside could have been torn upside down, with experienced investigators rousting drug dealers and pressing their informants. But that was never done. No one ever seemed to identify or question Sonny's junkie girlfriend, either.

Maybe the best question to be asked is: To what end? What would the cops have found if they went all *CSI*? A hero cop? A high-level casino exec? A famous trumpeter? No, that's not the way Ralph Lamb ran his town. It was best to keep things quiet.

In 1977 prosecutors charged Lamb with taking payoffs to finance his lifestyle, and even though a friendly jury acquitted him, he was turned out of office, never to return. I approached him several times for an interview during my reporting for this book, getting as close to the front door of his home for a pre-arranged meeting. We'd talked briefly on the phone, and although he was ailing, he seemed willing. But as I stood on his threshold, a nurse who answered his door told me he wasn't feeling up to it. At her suggestion I returned a few hours later, but nothing had changed. I called him for months afterward, to no avail. Lamb died in July 2015 without ever publicly shedding more light on the Liston case.

With so many other people from that era dying, the chance to find new evidence is rapidly shrinking. But there are still those who can help, including Rabbit Watkins, the former bellman who was close to Sonny.

On the day in May 2014 that I visited him at his home, Watkins was sitting in a living room that reeked of the gas oven, left open in the kitchen to heat the place. A situation comedy was playing full-blast on the television and he rocked back and forth in his recliner, chuckling out of sync with the jokes. The curtains were pulled tight.

Even though he knew what I'd come for, it took Watkins a while to warm to the subject, and me a while to understand what he was saying. He spoke quickly, giving up on most sentences halfway through. In an hourlong interview, however, there was one thing he was firm about: "That wasn't no accidental overdose."

I asked him why and he described meeting Jimmy Gay, the mortician whose job it was to get Sonny ready for his funeral. "He told me Sonny had a big hole in the back of his head," Watkins said, his eyes suddenly narrow and clear. "Sonny was murdered."

It may have been that Sonny's body was so badly decomposed, someone who handled it dug a finger into his head. But maybe not. It's one more lead that was never followed up on in a case that doesn't fit neatly in the museums Las Vegas is building these days.

Personally, I think the answer to what happened to Sonny Liston lies in a cemetery in Las Vegas. But it's not in Plot A-2-20 at Davis Memorial Park, where the headstone for Sonny Liston reads: *A Man*.

I think the answer lies ten miles to the east of there, in the Palm Mortuary on Boulder Highway, where Irwin Peters Jr. was laid to rest. Sonny wasn't the only one who went into the ground without a homicide investigation. Peters was pushed into his final resting place with just as many secrets.

The two deaths that occurred sixteen years and a thousand miles apart are regarded as accidents. But I don't think there was anything accidental about them. I believe that finding the killer of Irwin Peters will unravel the real story of what happened to Sonny Liston.

It will also open up a chapter of Las Vegas history that a lot of people would just as soon keep buried.

ACKNOWLEDGMENTS

There's been so much written about Las Vegas that I worried about breaking new ground. But from the moment my wife, Ellen, went to the New York Public Library and read through every edition of the *Las Vegas Sun* from 1970, I realized that we were sitting on a gold mine. She was the first and last curator of this book, and a blood-hound to boot.

I took a lot of guided tours through Las Vegas in my reporting. But none of them matched the history that Stan Armstrong was able to re-create on our walks through the Westside. Stan's father, Lloyd, was a butcher at the Ranch Market on Van Buren Street as well as a fight trainer, and he knew all the celebrities who lived in town, includ-ing Sonny. His intimate view of his city informs Stan's wonderful documentaries about the black experience in Las Vegas, among them

The Misunderstood Legend of the Las Vegas Moulin Rouge and *The Rancho High School Riots,* and many passages in this book.

The best writers in the business covered Sonny Liston through his tumultuous life, from Jimmy Breslin to James Baldwin. I'm lucky to call one of them, Bob Lipsyte, a friend. Bob is known for his opinion writing, most recently as an ombudsman for my employer, ESPN. But he's old-school when it comes to his reporting. He still has his original notebooks from the two Ali–Liston fights and graciously dragged them out to keep me honest. Another hero, Nick Pileggi, helped me understand the way Ralph Lamb ruled Vegas. Even though his CBS show about Lamb was short-lived, his book *Casino* remains a master class in chronicling the Vegas underworld.

In some respects, this book picks up where Nick Tosches left off in 2000 with *The Devil and Sonny Liston.* His take on Sonny is at once lyrical and investigative, and his analysis of the autopsy report, which exposed the fallacy of Syndrome X as a cause of death, is as definitive as these things get. I also turned to *Sonny Liston: The Real Story Behind the Ali-Liston Fights* by Paul Gallender. A nonprofit fund-raiser from Chicago, Gallender is the first to admit that he's not a reporter. But as a Liston fan, he spent thirty-five years researching his book—a remarkable achievement that helped get many essential voices on the record.

Other source books (and great reads) include: *Sonny Liston: The Champ Nobody Wanted* by A. S. "Doc" Young; *Brown Bomber: The Pilgrimage of Joe Louis* by Barney Nagler; *King of the World: Muhammad Ali and the Rise of an American Hero* by David Remnick; *Ali and Liston: The Boy Who Would Be King and the Ugly Bear* by Bob Mee; and *The Phantom Punch: The Story Behind Boxing's Most Controversial Bout* by Rob Sneddon.

I also relied on the magazine work of Bruce Jay Friedman, who traveled in the same circles as I did for *Esquire* but forty years earlier, and the great *Sports Illustrated* writers Robert Boyle, Tex Maule, Mark Kram, Barbara La Fontaine, and Bill Nack.

As for the rest of my source material, I've tried to be as transparent as possible, so a notes section seems superfluous. But I'd be happy to provide citations to anyone who asks. Feel free to e-mail listonbook@ gmail.com.

For this once-in-a-lifetime journey, I owe a deep debt to David Rosenthal of Blue Rider Press. David had my proposal for less than twenty-four hours when he bought it, and over the last few years he has kept me laser-focused on the original idea—especially when I had delusions of digressions. Best of all, he put me in the craftsmanlike hands of Brant Rumble, who doesn't do panic. Instead, he keeps the pages turning. Everyone at the David Black Agency, particularly Gary Morris, kept the train on the tracks.

A special round of thanks goes to my intrepid intern, Brent Martelli, for turning up obscure research at all hours in the University of Nevada library, and to David Schwartz in the Special Collections Division there, for guiding him. I'm also grateful to my cousin Brian for putting me up in the mountains of Henderson when I needed a hideout away from the Strip.

I've found that the best storytellers are usually cops. And even though the five-hour drive from Vegas to Ely, Nevada, was hairraising—I'd never been passed by a truck going 110 mph on a singlelane highway before, and I instantly understood why the vultures were circling—it was worth it to meet Gary Beckwith. After a lifetime of investigating dirty police officers, Beckwith left Vegas without looking back. But his memory of those years is still sharp and he's still fighting the war. "We had a lot of rat cops," he told me.

Not surprisingly, Beckwith didn't show up for a 2015 reunion of sheriff's deputies that included Ralph Lamb and Larry Gandy. "Make your calls now," Gandy wrote when he sent me a copy of the photo taken at the reunion. "Everyone's dying." Indeed, Lamb died just a few months after the photo was taken, as did Beckwith's old boss, Karl Albright, one of the first men on the scene of Sonny's death.

I've continued to exchange e-mails with Gandy since finishing this book, and it's clear that he's struggling to reconcile himself with what he's done. "I have a hard time sleeping but when I do, I have nightmares about my past," he wrote me in January 2016. Memories, he added, still come back to haunt him.

SHAUN ASSAEL
Wilmington, North Carolina

INDEX